A Portrait of Machy~~nlleth and its~~ Surroundings

by

Caradawc o Lancarfan

Translated by

Nicholas Islwyn Dugdale Fenwick

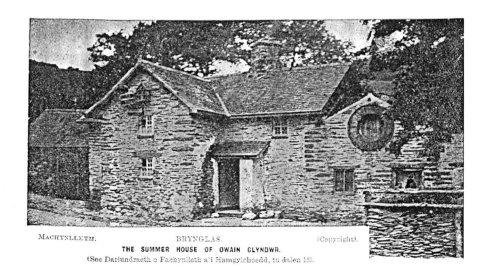

MACHYNLLETH.   BRYNGLAS.   (Copyright).
THE SUMMER HOUSE OF OWAIN GLYNDWR.
(See Darlundraeth o Fachynlleth a'i Hamgylchoedd, tu dalen 15).

First published by Adam Evans, Machynlleth, 1854
as *Darlundraeth O Fachynlleth A'i Hamgylchoedd*

First English edition 2009
© Nicholas Islwyn Dugdale Fenwick
All rights reserved

ISBN 978 1 904784 24 1

Published and distributed by

Coch-y-Bonddu Books

Machynlleth, Powys, SY20 8DG
Tel 01654 702837   Fax 01654 702857
www.anglebooks.co.uk

Printed in Great Britain by
the MPG Books Groups Group, Bodmin and King's Lynn

To my wife Elizabeth, my children Myfanwy and Morfudd, and my parents, Julian and Frances Fenwick

Nicholas Fenwick

INTRODUCTION

The postcard shown on the title page of this book is the earliest picture of which I am aware of Brynglas, the house in which my family and I live, and it was from this that I first became aware of the existence of *Darlundraeth o Fachynlleth a'i Hamgylchoedd*.

Having obtained a copy of the book, I could only agree with the praise given to the author in the original preface, and that I should also like to see it *"...translated skilfully into English, and to be made a handsome book, fit to put into the hand of a foreign traveller on a visit to the Principality"*. While I do not claim to be capable of such skilful translation, I trust that the significant advice and help I have received from a multitude of people has resulted in an English language version which is acceptable to the reader.

While parts of the content of the original book were clearly translated into Welsh from works such as Samuel Lewis's 1833 *Topographical Dictionary of Wales*, the author also succeeded in collecting and recording a great deal of information from local sources, and for this, if for nothing else, deserves great praise for having preserved so much information which would otherwise have been lost.

As alluded to in the preface, there are doubtless some portions of the original text that contain historical inaccuracies, while others, viewed with the benefit of current scientific and historical knowledge, might be branded as pure romance. Nevertheless, it is fair to say that this is more a reflection of the understanding of the period, rather than of the author's youth or ability, and such inaccuracies do not detract from the fascinating nature of much of the information contained in the book. Moreover, given his age at the time, and the fact that he was writing at the cusp of the social and cultural revolution that would accompany the coming of the railway to the region in 1863, the quality of his work stands as an early testament to a talent that would later have so much influence on Wales's history.

While I have not attempted to correct historical and other inaccuracies to any significant extent, I have added some notes of clarification and interest and distinguished these from the references contained in the original text by initialling them.

It should be noted that in translating those passages that the author himself translated from English, I did not return to the original sources, and there may therefore be discrepancies between these and my translations back into English. I also chose to preserve the author's original writing style as much as possible, rather than to re-write the book in modern English, and it is interesting to note that this has resulted in a style that does not differ significantly from English writings of the period. For similar reasons, I have preserved the author's original spellings of place-names and the like.

Notwithstanding the advice and guidance I have received from numerous people in relation to the translation of the main text, I am also indebted to Eurig Salisbury of the University of Wales's *Centre for Advanced Welsh and Celtic Studies*, Aberystwyth, for having provided translations of many of the poems contained herein, either by his own hand, or by tracing previous translations; in all cases the source of the translations are referenced.

Nicholas I D Fenwick

Brynglas, 17th April, 2009

ACKNOWLEDGEMENTS

I am indebted to the following people, listed in no particular order, for their advice during the production of this book:

Mirain Llwyd Owen (Caeathro), Alun Edwards (Rhyd y Main), David Wyn Jones (Garsiwn), Julian Fenwick (Machynlleth), Revd Harri Parri (Caernarfon), Bet Evans (Cwrt), Richard Knight Williams (Cheltenham).

I am also particularly indebted to David Meredith (Cwm Cynllwyd) for having edited the first draft, and to Gemma Davies (Tregaron) and Revd Richard Lewis (Bow Street) for their invaluable advice in terms of editing and amending the final draft.

I would also like to thank Paul Morgan of Coch-y-Bonddu books for undertaking to publish the book.

ABOUT THE AUTHOR

Evan Jones, who wrote *Darlundraeth o Fachynlleth a'i Hamgylchoedd* under the pseudonym *Caradawc o Lancarfan**, was born on the 27th of October 1836 at Esgair Goch, Pennal, to John Jones of Maestirau, Darowen, and his wife Catherine (née Jervis) of Llanbrynmair. He was baptised on November the 3rd by the Reverend Foulk Evans, minister of the Calvinistic Methodists at Capel Norton, Llynlloedd Lane, Machynlleth.

The family moved to Graigyrhenffordd, Penegoes, and it was arranged that Evan Jones enrol at the Machynlleth National School, where his sister was already a paying scholar, on the condition that he attend Sunday services in the Church at Penegoes. He later attended the non-conformist school at Graig Chapel, Machynlleth, under the instruction of minister Robert Griffiths. In 1849 he was apprenticed to Machynlleth printer and publisher Adam Evans, who in 1855 published *Darlundraeth o Fachynlleth a'i Hamgylchoedd,* which appears here as an English translation.

Between 1855 and 1857 Jones worked as a printer in Bethesda, and in the office of *Yr Herald Cymraeg* in Caernarfon, before entering into partnership with Lewis Jones, one of the founders of the Welsh settlement in Patagonia. In 1859 he returned to Machynlleth, where he set up as a printer and began to preach. In 1863 he entered Bala Calvinistic Methodists College, and in 1867 he became the pastor of chapels in Corris and Aberllefenni. While at Corris he married Jane Elizabeth Jones, daughter of Robert Jones of Bala, with whom he had two daughters and a son.

------

* The original *Caradawc,* or *Caradoc, o Lancarfan (Caradoc of Llancarfan)*, was a monk at Llancarfan monastery, near Cowbridge, Glamorgan, during the 12th century, and a contemporary of Geoffrey of Monmouth. He is most noted as the author of the *Life of Gildas*, a 6th Century British Saint (NIDF)

Evan Jones, circa 1870
(Published courtesy of Gwasg Pantycelyn)

Evan Jones* was ordained in 1869, and in 1872 became a minister in Dyffryn Ardudwy, before being made pastor of Moriah, Caernarfon, in 1875, where he remained until his retirement in 1906.

During his life, he became one of the most prominent leaders of the Welsh nonconformist movement, and established a reputation as a journalist, publisher, and formidable political opponent in any

---

* See *'Yr Hen Barchedig' – Portread o Anghydffurfiwr – Evan Jones, Caernarfon* by Harri Parri, Gwasg Pantycelyn (2004)

debate. He was moderator of the North Wales Methodist Association in 1897, moderator of the General Assembly in 1898-9, the principal founder of the Calvinistic Methodist Bookroom, and in 1909 was the first Welshman to be made president of the National Free Church Council.

During his period in Corris, Jones contributed weekly Welsh articles to *The Cambrian News,* a selection of which were published in 1905 and 1912, in books entitled *Ysgrifau Byrion.* In 1872 he became editor of *Y Goleuad,* a position which he held for four years, and in his later years he wrote a weekly article for that paper. He wrote for the *Genedl Gymreig* for a number of years, and in 1882 established *Yr Amseroedd,* which he later transferred to another proprietor. Between 1900 and 1905 he edited *Y Drysorfa,* and his reminiscences were published in 1912-13 in *Y Genedlin.*

Upon his retirement *The Christian Life* described him as a *'fierce preacher',* stating that *'He is a distinguished Welshman. One would be glad if England knew him better',* and John Puleston Jones described him as *'a great preacher, a very great preacher'.*

David Wyn Davies

Tanerdy, Machynlleth, 9th August, 2009

xi

Esgair Goch, near Pennal, where Evan Jones was born

PREFACE

Early in the year 1854, the Machynlleth Literary Society offered a small prize for the *"Best Portrait of Machynlleth and its Surroundings"*, but nobody felt it in their hearts to seize upon the subject of the competition except the composer of the following essay. The judges deemed the author worthy of the prize, and on their strong recommendation it is allowed to appear through the press.

It is fair to publicise the fact that the author rewrote and added a great deal to it after it came into the possession of the judges, and he reformed those errors that were noted, and that he considered to be errors.

Despite this, we are aware that there are a large multitude of defects and failings, and we appeal for clemency for these from those readers who feel keen to get the measure of it, for apart from numerous considerations:

1. The prize was only very small for a subject of such import.

2. There were barely six months in which to compose the portrait.

3. The difficulties faced by the author; he had not reached his 18th year, and had not served his term as apprentice, and so only had such time as he could steal from proper leisure and sleep towards its completion. And when we add to this the lack of means to purchase proper books for the task, the local stability of his calling, in combination with the huge obstructions to obtaining information about the various places he was unfamiliar with, we are confident that the sensible and sympathetic will not behave cruelly towards him.

We wish to acknowledge with thanks the prompt assistance received at the hand of a multitude of friends who felt an interest in the work, and especially to my sincere friend Lewis Glyn Dyfi, to whom we are indebted for a great deal of information.

It only remains for it to be presented to the attention of our compatriots, with the hope that it will be gratefully received, and that the publisher will be compensated for his effort to serve his country. And if it raises a new desire in someone to trace the history of the house in which they live, or the town in which they reside, or the parish they belong to, and to take note of the events which took place in those places in the times of their predecessors, for the sake of interest and education, we would regard that as enough repayment for the trouble taken to write it.

Yours humbly

IEUAN DYFI

Machynlleth, January 20th, 1855

THE ADJUDICATION

Portrait of Machynlleth and its surroundings by *"Caradawc o Lancarfan"*

As the above composition is the only one which has been presented in competition for the 4th Prize of the *"Machynlleth Literary Society"*, the task of adjudication has been very easy, particularly as it is also a production of far greater merit than I ever expected it should have been. Indeed, with a few corrections and additions, it will form a very valuable and meritorious record of whatever is noteworthy in connection with the place and neighbourhood indicated. It is very well written, and the information given of the history, production, produce, trade, etc. of the district, reflects great credit upon the author's industry, research, and local knowledge of the district.

The account given of the political and other transactions of this portion of Central Wales is very full, as far as regards the latter portion of the historical period, being chiefly deficient in relation to the pre-historic and early historical annals of the place.
The same remark also holds true in regard to its Geology and Natural History – a region of knowledge which the author does not seem to have explored or studied deeply.
The author has also not paid proper attention to the dividing of words.

I am also not satisfied as to the correctness of the derivation of the term *"Machynlleth"* as therein given, as, in my opinion, the word is compounded of *"Mach-cyn-llaeth"*, a sure place for producing the first or best milk. The vale of Machynlleth was one of the chief milking stations of the Ardyfeich, or Ordovices. Glan-mach-los and cilfach (cil-mach) are words of similar composition, and seemingly signify a grazing station, or small plain hedged in by hills.

It is hardly correct to say that Penhelyg forms a *"rhan helaeth"* *("large portion")* of Aberdovey; more properly it is a separate Village, adjacent to but separate from Aberdovey.

"Brodyr" would be a more correct term than *"Plymouth Brethren"*, as the congregation so called by the author is in no way connected with the *"Plymouth Brethren"*, though established on somewhat similar principles perhaps.

The author also omits to mention that the eminent Lewis Morris, the patron of the great Goronwy Owen, was collector of Aberdovey. *"Brenin Ieuan"* is given instead of *"Brenin Ioan"*, who really signed the *"Magna Carta"*.

"Gwyddno Garanhir" is incorrectly rendered *"Gwyddno Goronhir"*. Seithinyn Fedw is said to have *"forgotten to close the flood-gates of Cantref y Gwaelod"*, and not to have *purposely* opened them. Let the devil have his due.

The probable situation of *"Castell Dyfi"* was Bryn Celwydd.

Tref-rydd, (the wanderer's home) was the abode of a noted free-booter in the reign of Henry IV, and was liberated through the influence of his neighbour, Jenkin Vaughan of Caethle – Vide Bank.

The true meaning of *"nant"*, the author does not seem to apprehend, as many others do not. It signifies a hollow formed by a small stream.

I do not think that Corris signifies *"grisiau defaid" ("sheep steps")*. Rather it signified *"Cor-ris"*, a very high step or gris.

"Aber" is also misunderstood: it signifies the confluence of a stream.

The author is also sometimes at fault in grammar. But upon the whole, I am glad to say that his production well deserves a *better* Prize than the one given; and of his work and labour I think so highly, that I shall be glad to subscribe for five copies when it is printed. I think, if it were rendered into English by a competent hand, it would be highly esteemed by visitors, as it excels in a kind of information in which Welsh Guide Books are very deficient.

JOHN PUGHE
Society lecturer for County of
Merioneth to the Cambrian
Archaeological Association

Penhelyg House, September 2ⁿᵈ, 1854

I read *"A Portrait of Machynlleth and its Surroundings"* and did not think that it would be possible to obtain such material, nor that it would be possible to collect such a whole history of the place, and make it such an interesting one. It is very praiseworthy of the candidate for the prize that he has written so extensively, and given such a complete history of the town, the villages, and other noteworthy places close to it, so tidily, and considering the assistance available to him.

I think if it were printed, young readers with a taste for reading would be very keen to buy it. If it were turned to English, I do not have the slightest doubt that it would be a means to attract to the place more attention than it has ever had, because the English frequently ask whether there is a *"guide book"* available that includes the history of the place and its surroundings in connection with the fact that the town is a place where Owain Glyndwr dwelt and held his parliament. Here is material for a book, I imagine, that would correct that deficiency.

I hope to see it again translated skilfully into English, and to be made a handsome book, fit to put into the hand of a foreign traveller on a visit to the Principality. The history and its recounts from other localities, such as Aberdyfi, etc., show a great taste in the candidate to collect history that is useful to know. I wonder, impartially, whether if one started reading it, it would not be put down before going through it all. I wish, if it can be published, to recommend it heartily to the attention of the public.

JOHN THOMAS
Pharmacist
Machynlleth, December, 1854

A PORTRAIT

MACHYNLLETH

This is the main town in the westerly part of Trafaldwyn county (Montgomeryshire). It stands on a small agreeable plain, with two hills rising on each side, within around half a mile of the River Dyfi, which is tidal to Derwenlas, within two miles of the town.

The distances from the main surrounding towns are as follows:

Llundain (London)	206	miles
Caerlleon (Chester)	70	"
Amwythig (Shrewsbury)	57	"
Drefnewydd (Newtown)	28	"
Llanidloes	20	"
Aberystwyth	18	"
Dolgellau	17	"
Towyn	14	"

Although it has not kept a prominent place in the register of history, it has not completely escaped attention.

It is commonly assumed that it is one and the same as the Romans' *Maglona* in which, during the time of the Emperor Honorius, the captain of the *Numerius Solensium* lived, along with a strong army for the purpose of keeping the male inhabitants of these areas under the yoke of the Romans.

It is said that there was a strong castle or fortress raised on a hill behind the town, in association with another strong camp, *Cefncaer*, near Pennal, and that a stone road was made from the fortress through the damp plains below the town, to the base of a small hill by Pen-y-ddol, and that most of the old church of Machyn-

1

Machynlleth in the early 19th Century (top), and now (bottom)

lleth* was built from the stones of this road. Having performed a precise inspection on the hill of Penrallt, I do not have enough evidence presently to establish this beyond doubt; but if such a place existed, the most likely place for it I can establish is the top of the cliff called Gallt y Gog. On the highest part of this hill is a plateau in the shape of a circle, and this does not appear dissimilar to the base of an old castle. From here we can see a full view of the whole country around, and, as a result, the place was advantageous to perceive the movements of enemies. Numerous coins bearing the seals of some of Rome's Emperors have also been found around this place.

After the Romans were called from this island to defend their own country, we get hardly any history about the town until the time of Henry IV, when we see...

> -------------- *Llew Glyndwr*
> *Yn arwain ei arfogion dewr i'r gad,*
> *I roi ar ffo elynion blin fy ngwlad.*

> -------------- *Glyndwr's lion*
> *Leading his brave soldiers to battle*
> *To put to flight the evil enemies of my country*

Since the history of this man is so connected with our town, we are confident that this will be excuse enough for giving a few notes about him here.

In relation to the birth of Owain ab Gruffydd Fychan, or, as we know him conventionally, Owain Glyndwr, there is some disagreement in the records: Some establish it as having been on the 28th of May

---

* See "Lewis's Topographical Dictionary of Wales", "Cliff's Book of North Wales" and "Williams' Geiriadur"

1354, while others have it five years earlier, in 1349, which is notable due to the arrival of a dreadful disease. Historians say, in order to make the tradition more noteworthy, that his father's stallions were found standing in the stables up to their bellies in blood the night Owain was born, interpreting this as an indication of his bloodthirsty and warmongering inclination.

Regarding the place where he was born, it is stated in old writings in the possession of the late Reverend Mr Pugh, Tygwyn, in Dinbych county (Denbighshire), that this happened in a place called Tref-garn, in Penfro county (Pembrokeshire); but because farms and parishes of this name exist in both counties, it is not easy to establish which of these was his birth-place.

He could boast abundantly in terms of his blood, inasmuch as his lineage ran through some of the most famous families of the nation, and from Royal blood on both his father's and mother's side. Three Welsh Royal dynasties came together in him, namely that of Bleddyn ab Cynfyn, from Powys, Rhys ab Tewdwr, from the South, and Gruffydd ab Cynan, from Gwynedd; it is this that establishes his legal right to the crown of Gwalia*.

We do not have any history of his youth, but it is likely that he had an education suited to his wealth and pedigree. His education was completed in one of the highest legal courts as a diligent student of English law, and he doubtless won several verbal victories before appearing in the field as a warrior. We cannot say whether he held office, but he was talked of highly in terms of his situation to Sir David Hanmer, one of the Sovereign court judges, who gave Glyndwr his daughter as wife, who bore him numerous children.

Our hero's name appears as a witness in a dispute relating to a Coat of Arms between Sir Richard Scrope and Sir Robert Le Grosvenor in 1386, as *"Owain, Lord Glyndwr, aged 22"*, which must be a mistake

---

* Gwalia: An old name for Wales, or the lands inhabited by the Welsh, which were formerly more expansive (NIDF)

for 32. We can form an opinion regarding his character and his upbringing from the following words that the English bard composed for him:

> *Glendower. 'I can speak English, lord, as well as you,*
> *For I was trained up in the English court:*
> *Where being but young, I framed to the harp*
> *Many an English ditty, lovely well,*
> *And gave the tongue a helpful ornament.'*

First Part Henry IV. Act iii. Sc. 1

At some time during his youth he lived with Earl Arundel, after which it is likely he went to serve the Royal Family. He came into special favour with Richard II, and this man made him a bearer to him in his wars in France and Ireland, as well as in his civil wars, and Richard rewarded him for his bravery and unique loyalty by ordaining him a Knight. However, it does not appear that he ever used this title after his retreat to Wales, which occurred after the deposition of Richard in 1399 and the ascension of Henry IV to the throne.

Although Owain officiated for the King, his duties did not prevent him from spending part of each year on his estates in Wales. He had two extensive heirdoms; Glyndyfrdwy, in Meirionnydd (Merionethshire), and Sycharth, in Dinbych county (Denbighshire), with dwellings at both places. Here the bards championed to welcome him, saying

> *Myned, mae adduned ddain,*
> *Lles yw, tua llys Owain.*
>
> . . .

I'r llys ar ddyfrys ydd af,
O deucant odidocaf.
Llys barwn, lle syberwyd,
Lle daw beirdd am le da byd.

      . . .

Sycharth, buarth y beirdd.

A very great pilgrimage is going,
It is beneficial, towards Owain's court;

      . . .

I will go to his court in haste,
The most splendid of the two hundred;
A baron's court, place of refinement,
Where many poets come, place of the good life;

      . . .

Sycharth, enclosure of the poets.[1]

His residence is portrayed as

Tai Napl ar fold deunawplas,
Tŷ pren glân mewn top bryn glas,
Ar bedwar piler eres
Ei lys ef i nef yn nes;
Ar ben pob piler pren praff,
Lloft ar dalgrofft adeilgraff.
Naw neuadd, cofladd cynfun,
A naw wardrobe ar bob un.

Nine-plated buildings on the scale of eighteen mansions,
Fair wooden buildings on top of a green hill;
On four wonderful pillars
His court is nearer to heaven;

On top of each stout wooden pillar
A loft built firmly on the summit of a croft,
Nine symmetrical identical halls,
And nine wardrobes by each one,[1]

And of his hospitality that

Anodd yn fynych yno,
Weled na chlicied na chlo,
Na phorthoriaeth ni waeth neb,
Ni bydd eisiau budd oseb,
Na gwall, na newyn, na gwarth,
Na syched fyth yn Sycharth.

Very rarely was bolt or lock
To be seen there,
Nor did anyone act as porter;
There will be no want, beneficial gift,
Nor lack nor hunger nor shame,
Nor ever thirst in Sycharth.[1]

But the most pleasant morning was seen to precede the most harsh day, and despite the quality of the friendship between Owain and the Royal Family, they now became enemies. During the reign of Richard II a fierce legal dispute occurred between Owain and Rheinallt, Lord Grey, from Rhuthin, in relation to a common called Croesau, which lay between the Lordships of Rhuthin and Glyndyfrdwy.

The legal dispute was won by Glyndwr at that time, but in the first year of Henry IV's reign the proud and covetous Lord of Rhuthin seized the said common, judging that Owain had no backing following the dethronement of his patron, and therefore would be more inclined to support Grey's objective.

This would have been enough of an incitement to anger one with a less fiery temper than our hero; yet despite his honour he did not raise arms to defend his rights before making every effort to solve the quarrel by gentler means; he brought a complaint before Parliament, but totally unsuccessfully. John Trefor, the Bishop of Llanelwy, told Parliament that Owain's complaint was not to be disregarded, because it was likely that if it was not given attention, Wales would bear arms. The only answer he got was *"What care we for barefoot rascals?"*

Lord Grey's step of arrogance towards this Welshman was not enough; he also had to tarnish his honour at the first opportunity he got by portraying him as one who might be unfaithful to the King; for when King Henry was starting out on a campaign against the Scots, he summoned his Barons and their armies to follow, and amongst others there was Owain. But unfortunately the King's writ was given to Lord Grey to convey to Owain, and he kept it so late that it was not possible for Owain to appear with the other Barons.

Henry attributed this to insubordination and deliberate disloyalty, this being made even more credible through misportrayal by Lord Grey, and as a result *"Glyndwr"* was pronounced a traitor, and his possessions forfeit; with this as an excuse, Lord Grey overran some of Glyndwr's heirdoms.

By now the anger that would have been long building up in the bosom of our hero was beginning to break out – he could not suffer the insult cast upon him and his nation any longer, and he prepared to protect himself. This is how the rebellion that lasted fifteen years, and cost 100,000 men their lives, started.

---

* Woodward's Wales, vol. ii., p.565

Owain's first deed done by way of revenging this injustice was to muster a few brave Welshmen from around him and, once armed, repossess his heirdoms and take possession, through excessive force, of Lord Grey's lands, while Grey was at the Royal Court. After this, Lord Grey and Lord Talbot came with an army of Royal soldiers to attack him, and they almost caught him, but he somehow succeeded in escaping to a nearby wood, where he hid for a time.

By now totally convinced that there was no longer any mercy or justice to be expected at the hand of the King, who decided to completely destroy him in order to honour Lord Grey, Glyndwr mustered a troop of good willed, brave and armed men, and on the day of Rhuthin Fair, the 20th of September 1400, he led them to the aforementioned town and burnt the larger part of it, plundering hugely and killing many of the inhabitants, as well as the English merchants who came to the fair. Once Owain had finished this task, he retreated to the mountains to hide in some of their inaccessible defences to gather more of his fellow men under his banner*.

This news spread like wildfire throughout the whole of Wales until there was turmoil everywhere, and hosts from all quarters enlisted under Owain's banner, and they began to call him the *"Prince of Wales"*. The bards also did their part to nurse the spirit by recalling the old bardic prophesies that had rolled from age to age, addressing him as *"the prophesised son"*, and so on, until a passionate flame of patriotism and independence among the nation was ignited. In him, they expected someone who would reclaim their freedom and country, and take complete revenge on their oppressors.

When King Henry heard this, he summoned the whole military power of the ten counties of England to take with him to Wales in order to curb the rebels; but Owain was too cunning to bring his

---

* Darlithiau ar Hanes y Cymry, by O. Jones, page 245-247

men to the field against the might of Henry; he stayed in the nooks of the mountains, watching all the movements of the King's army like an eagle, and the King had to return in shame without being any nearer to putting down the rebellion.

On November the 8th 1400, Henry sold the skin before catching the bear: He gave as a present to his brother, the Earl of Somerset, all the heirdoms of Owain in North and South Wales. The rents at that time were paid in goods, but the new Lord did not have the capacity to take possession, and so the land-holders were left alone.

On the 30th of November an announcement came from the King that was quite different from those that had come before; he offered to *"take into his protection every Welshman who came to Caerlleon (Chester) offering submission to his son Henry"*, but very few accepted the offer. He also abolished many old laws placed upon us as a nation at the time of our humiliation.

Nothing especially happened at the beginning of 1401. Owain was making every effort to further his cause, and was receiving the energetic cooperation of his fellow countrymen; the Welsh labourers and craftsmen were seen to come to him from all parts of the Kingdom, exchanging the plough for the sword, and the beam of the loom for the lance. The Welsh students at the Universities left their books to go to fight – all credit to them – for their freedom and their country.

Since Owain had lands and good benefactors in North and South Wales, he decided to set up his camp on Pumlummon, a high mountain near the borders of the two regions. From here, he launched destructive attacks on the castles, towns, and local villages. He burnt Trallwm (Welshpool), Abbey Cwmhir, and the castle of Maelienydd*.

The positions of Owain's encampments were very advantageous:

---

* Maelienydd Castle is commonly known as Cefnllys Castle, and is 3 miles east of Llandrindod Wells (NIDF)

"His handful of men could, being defended within their strong soldierly ditches, repel the whole might of the Marcher Lords, but possessed a good abundance of food and provisions for war within his camp" [*].

From here, Owain would take his men and raid the Flemish who inhabited Dyfed and Ceredigion, harassing them bitterly, and in the end they decided to make a fair attempt at putting an end to his attacks. They gathered fifteen-hundred armed men, and surrounded Glyndwr and part of his army on the mountain of Hyddgant[†]. The fact that they were caught like this shows that a careful watch was not being kept; but anyone can get into difficulty - the capability is shown by getting out of it.

Seeing that he and his few men – around two- or three-hundred in number – had no path by which to escape except by breaking their way through the ranks, they rushed upon the Flemish, and thereby broke through their ranks, leaving more than two-hundred of their men dead on the field, and driving the rest into flight, as if a troop of fiends had attacked them.

This success elevated Owain's fame marvellously; the people swarmed to him, and his name terrified near and far away. At around this time, having been frightened by Owain Glyndwr, Henry IV came with his armies to conquer Wales once more; he burnt the spectacular monastery of Ystrad Fflur (Strata Florida), laying waste the surrounding countryside. But there was no need for the Welsh to fight; the elements were fighting on their behalf, and without winning anything to ease the tiredness of the campaign, Henry led his exhausted and scattered army back to England.

At this time a number of Welsh peers became insincere towards Owain. In an historical Act at Westminster, on July the 8th 1401, favourable pardon was given by the King to William ab Tudur and

---

[*] Darlithiau ar Hanes y Cymry, page 248
[†] Now known as "Hyddgen" (NIDF)

11

thirty-one Welsh nobles*. But the army of our leader was too strong a presence to be disheartened by this. In the following autumn, Henry and his hosts came again to Wales, but unsuccessfully.

At the beginning of the year 1402 a comet appeared†, and this influenced the thoughts of the superstitious multitudes in a favourable way for Owain and his cause. Iolo Goch composed a *cywydd*‡ poem on this fact, saying

> *Beth yw'r seren, boeth awel?*
> *Myfi a ŵyr lwyr loyw-ryw,*
> *Deall hyn, a dillyn yw:-*
> *Dur yw ei phaladr, neu dân,*
> *A draig i'r Mab Darogan.*

> *What manner of star is she, hot gust?*
> *It is I who know, so bright her nature,*
> *I understand this, she is beautiful:-*
> *Steel is her stem, or fire,*
> *And a dragon for the Son of Prophecy.²*

Glyndwr led his army to Henffordd§ county (Herefordshire), burning and spoiling. Sir Edmund Mortimer came to meet him, and a battle was fought on the 22ⁿᵈ of June at Bryn-glas, a mountain

---

* Welsh Sketches, third series, page 63
† On the 20ᵗʰ of February 1402 a comet appeared to the east of Pisces/Andromeda whose rays pointed eastwards. It was visible in daylight for eight days, and was visible for two months in all (NIDF)
‡ A cywydd is a poem consisting of a series of seven-syllable lines in rhyming couplets. One of the lines must finish with a stressed syllable, while the other must finish with an unstressed syllable (NIDF)
§ Henffordd – from which Hereford gets its name; hen ffordd = old road (NIDF)

near Pilleth, Radnorshire. The Welshmen in Mortimer's army were not willing to fight against Owain, for although they loved their Lord well, they loved their country better. The majority fled at the first strike, and the rest – the archers – turned against their own side. 1,100 Henffordd (Hereford) men were killed, and Mortimer was taken prisoner. Shakespeare appropriately said

> *There came*
> *A post from Wales, loaden with heavy news;*
> *Whose worst was, that the noble Mortimer,*
> *Leading the men of Herefordshire to fight*
> *Against the irregular and wild Glendower,*
> *Was by the rude hands of that Welshman taken,*
> *And a thousand of his people butchered*

Owain's arch-enemy, Lord Grey, prepared to attack him, deciding to bring his galling pomposity to an eternal head. But Owain understood this, and instead of staying on the defensive, and waiting for his enemy to make the first strike, he led his men to the neighbourhood of Rhuthin, and, having prepared a plot, he succeeded in taking Lord Grey as prisoner. But, to his credit, instead of killing Grey on the spot, he kept him prisoner for several months in Eryri (Snowdonia), and in the end released him on the condition that ten-thousand marks would be paid, each one being equivalent to two guineas in current terms. After this, Grey married one of Owain's daughters, and did not raise his hand against him again.

Having won such victory over his main enemy, Owain turned to take revenge on some of his main compatriots who were favourable towards King Henry. He plundered the heirdoms of Ieuan ab Meredydd from Eifionydd, and especially Trefor, the Bishop of Llanelwy. It is apparent that at around this time Owain killed his relative, Hywel Sele of Nannau, and hid him in *"Ceubren yr Ellyll"*

(*"Hollow Tree of the Ghoul"*)[*], about which there is abundant tradition in the areas around Dolgellau – but it serves no purpose for us to include these here. By now Henry was making a repeat campaign against Wales, and came with three strong armies; one camped at Henffordd (Hereford), one at Amwythig (Shrewsbury), and the other at Caerlleon (Chester), in order to attack the Welsh from as many points as possible at once. But Owain was open-eyed enough to withdraw to the mountains, driving in front of him the cattle and sheep which were grazing on the lowlands.

On came the English without meeting any obstacle or check apart from the wind and the rain that blew into their faces, and the mirey bogs which sunk under their feet. As they were travelling there was some terrible dread over them; were they perhaps in those valleys where the magicians ruled? Every stone was, in their minds, some reason to be afraid. In the devilish sound of the tempest and agitated rushing of the waters, they heard the wails of ghouls and the mocking laughter of devils.

"Give me flesh and blood to fight against and I shall not complain" was the secret thought of many a brave hearted Englishman *"But I am not going to compete against the powers of darkness"*[†]. So Henry had to return in the midst of failure and shame, consoling himself only by associating this with the wizardry of the enemy, rather than his ability and bravery. It was this that the Bard of Avon referred to in the words he placed on Owain's lips:

---

[*] Hywel Sele's corpse is said to have remained in the hollow trunk of what later became known as *Ceubren yr Ellyll (the ghoul's hollow trunk)* for many decades, and the tree was regarded as being haunted. The tree blew down during a storm on the night of the 13th of July 1813. Its trunk was found to measure 27 feet in circumference 3 feet from the ground. Its site, in the kitchen garden of Nannau, is marked by a sundial and a brass plate, on which is engraved a sketch of the tree (NIDF)

[†] Welsh Sketches, third series, page 72

14

I can call the spirits from the vasty deep

And it is likely that it was this retreat of Henry's to which he alluded in the following lines:

Three times did Henry Bollingbroke make head
Against the Welsh; thrice from the banks of the Wye,
And sandy-bottom'd Severn, did they send
Him bootless back, and weather beaten home

In this year, 1402, a quarrel occurred between the honourable Northumberland and Douglas families, in the north of England, and these sent a despatch to Glyndwr to try and get him to ally with them against the King, and this was consented to easily. In order to confirm this alliance, as well as to plan their actions in advance, young Percy, the son of the Earl of Northumberland, met Owain and Sir Edmund Mortimer, who was by now released and had thrown in his lot with the Welsh, in Aberdaron, in the house of Dafydd ab Daron, the Dean of Bangor*. They decided to share the Kingdom between them: Sir Edmund Mortimer, on behalf of his nephew, Earl March, was to have the land between the Trent and thc Severn, as far as the southern coast of the island; Earl Northumberland would have that part of the island north of the Trent, and Owain, in addition to the Principality of Wales, which he claimed as his birthright, would have the part to the west of the Severn.

Having searched, the learned found in writings by Merlin, who was considered to be a prophet, prophesies that the natural inheritors of the crown would perish under swift decision, and that the dragon, the lion and the wolf would share the Kingdom. The inheritor of the crown was Henry IV, who was *"accursed by the mouth of God*

---

* Mem. Of Owain Glyndwr, page 106

15

himself". Glyndwr was the dragon, taken from Uther, an imaginary leader, who bore this signal as an image; the lion was the head of the Percy family; and the wolf, it is supposed, was the coat of arms of Mortimer[*]. The analogy from the prophecy, and what had already taken place, had the effect of strengthening the thoughts of the confederates beyond doubt that their success was assured.

In this year, 1402, with the purpose of trying to get his fellow countrymen to accord with his work to bring upon himself the Royal authority of the Principality, Owain summoned a general Assembly to appear in Machynlleth. The nobles came together, and his title as the Prince of Wales was formally recognised, and even the ceremony of crowning him was completed; and the most sincere union was revealed in those present to recognise his rights, and to cooperate vigorously with him.

But in their midst was the traitor Sir Dafydd Gam[†], who, in the guise of supporting the universal objective, came to Machynlleth with the actual intention of killing Owain, so completing Henry's objectives, of whom he was a cordial supporter, and perhaps revenging the injury that he himself, or his kin, had suffered during some of the previous campaigns of the Prince to Henffordd (Hereford) and Maesyfed (Radnor)[‡]. But his wicked intention was discovered as it was about to be put into action; the traitor was caught, and would

---

[*] Pennant App. 349
[†] Dafydd Gam's full name was Dafydd Gam ap Llewelyn ap Hywel Fychan ap Hywel ap Einion Sais. Gam means cripple or bent. Gam died on October the 25th 1415 at the battle of Agincourt. His grandson was William Herbert, 1st Earl of Pembroke (1423-1469) (NIDF)
[‡] Tradition has it that Sir Dafydd Gam asked permission to converse with Owain in person; and our hero, not imagining that he meant any malice, granted this. While the two were in the room alone, Sir Dafydd took out a dagger that he had concealed in his outer garments and attempted to stab Owain; but our leader, through his strength and ability, succeeded in preventing the traitor from carrying out the hideous slaughter, and through this his life was saved.

16

have been put to death on the spot if it were not for some of the Prince's bosom friends speaking for him; he was instead imprisoned safely in the castle-house of Glyndyfrdwy[*]. Dafydd was in this prison for ten years[†‡], but in the end, in 1412, after the King sent messages to Owain to reach an agreement for his release, he was freed. Dafydd immediately launched an angry attack, which incensed the Prince so greatly that he took a host from Machynlleth, or, as they were known, the *"Children of the Garsiwn"* to the county of Radnor, and burnt Sir Dafydd's house in anger. One of his servants was caught, and Owain told him

> *Os gweli di ŵr coch Cam,*
> *Yn 'mofyn am Gyrnigwen,*
> *Dywed ei bod hi dan y lan,*
> *A nod y glo ar ei phen*

> *If you see a crooked red man*
> *Asking about Cyrnigwen[§],*
> *Say she is under the bank*
> *With the mark of coal on her head*

The traitor nevertheless escaped from the destruction wrought on him to England, where he remained in honour in the palace of

---

[*] Darlithiau ar Hanes y Cymry, 249
[†] Welsh Sketches, third series, 90
[‡] Given Gam's recorded participation in the Battle of Pwll Melyn in 1405, it seems unlikely that he was imprisoned for such a long period.
[§] Cyrnigwen is thought to have been the name of one of Dafydd Gam's forts, on the banks of the River Honddu. His main residence is thought to have been Hengwrt, a moated manor house near Llantilio Crossenny, Monmouthshire. A stained glass window in the church at Llantilio Crossenny bears the inscription *David Gam, golden haired knight, Lord of the manor of Llantilio Crossenny, killed on the field of Agincourt 1415* (NIDF)

Henry V*.

The house in which this parliament was held can be seen to this day in Maengwyn Street, but it has undergone many alterations. It is said that the stairs behind it lead to the main room, in which there were all sorts of decorative carvings, etc.[†] It is not easy for a Welshman to pass it without feeling solemn when it is remembered that this is the place where the last of the Welsh Princes was crowned. Here was the last offering to regain inherent possession of our privileges, and with his fall the small spark of our independence was extinguished for ever. From the outside a stone gateway was built, and as the alterations were made it was necessary to take the old gatehouse down. Nevertheless, the patriotic, kind, and generous gentleman, the late Sir John Edwards, Plâs, Machynlleth, was kind enough to go to the great expense of moving it to another place without its disintegration. He succeeded in doing this, and it endured to rest on the side of a beautiful house on the street as a monument to what was done in our town by our brave ancestors while struggling for their freedom. The respect of the inhabitants and visiting gentry towards the old *relic* was considerable. But it must be said with grief, *"the old monument is no more!"* Its antiquity and dignity failed to keep it up; for it was completely destroyed like an accursed thing, despite the wound to the multitudes.

It is apparent that Machynlleth was a place of considerable commerce at that time. It is likely from the old houses here that honourable gentlemen lived in the town in Owain's time. One of these old houses is at the top end of Maengwyn Street. It is of quite early construction. On its outside is a row of letters; and they have so far scorned every effort to decipher them; but the most usual

---

* Panorama of North Wales, 232
† Parry's Cambrian Mirror, 237

18

opinion is that they are the name of Owain Glyndwr*.

A sturdy, tall, and strong tree grew in front of this house, and, referring to this, the following lines are often heard being recited.

> *Dyma fon yr Onen fawr;*
> *Ned Rhys Huws a'i torodd i lawr*
>
> *Here lies the stump of the great Ash tree,*
> *It was Ned Rhys Huws who cut it down*

In Penrallt Street, a little way from the house next to the Wynnstay Arms[†], on the corner as you go to the Garsiwn, there is another quite ancient form, with special antiquity associated with it. It is not often that such a house is seen; from one end to the other and on the gable next to the street is the coat of arms of Owain carved beautifully in wood, and apparently it was here that his heroes dwelt[‡]. Tradition also has it that an underground way reaches this house from the Cefncaer camp, in Pennal, and that a penny candle gives enough light to go from one end to the other. When Charles I was on his journey through this area of Wales, it is said that he slept in this town in a place called the 'Garrison', the name to this day for that part of the town that is below this house, and it is beyond doubt that it was here he lodged. The bed in which he slept is kept safe in

---

*It might be assumed that the house referred to is 106 Maengwyn Street, which has carved on it " 𝖨𝟼𝟸𝟪𝗂𝟢 𝖶 𝖤𝖭·𝖯 𝖵 𝖰𝖧𝖨𝟢𝖵𝖷𝟢𝗋", interpreted by David Wyn Davies as "1628 OWEN PUGH UXOR" – i.e. *1628 Owen Pugh and his wife*, in which case, it is peculiar that the author describes these as having *"scorned every effort to decipher them"*(NIDF)

† The Wynnstay Arms referred to here is now a newsagents shop, located behind the town clock (NIDF)

‡ Dendrochronological dating has revealed that the main roof timbers of this building were felled in 1560/61, while those in the extension along the lane leading to the Garsiwn date from 1576 (NIDF)

19

Esgair Llyfirin*, on the way to Corris†.

But to return to the history of Owain; Percy and Douglas gathered their armies – around twelve-thousand men – and moved them towards the borders of Wales to meet Glyndwr. Henry rushed to oppose the rebels, and succeeded in coming between Percy and Owain before they could join. Henry occupied the land between Croesoswallt (Oswestry) and Amwythig (Shrewsbury), and Percy had to fight with him alone in a place near Amwythig (Shrewsbury), on the 21st of June, where Henry was victorious. Around two-thousand six-hundred nobles and gentry, most from the army of the King, and six thousand ordinary soldiers, two-thirds of whom were from Percy's army, were killed. Percy himself was killed, as well as Sir Jenkin Hamer, Owain's brother in law. Earls Worcester and Douglas were taken prisoner; the first was executed, but on the intervention of the King's son, more lenient demeanour was shown to Douglas. So Owain and his countrymen's plans were complicated, and he had to turn to his old work of pillaging territories and despoiling the belongings of the Marcher Lords.

At the beginning of 1404 Owain formed an alliance with the King of France. This alliance was confirmed and signed in Paris, on the 14th of June 1404, and was accepted by Owain in Llanbadarn castle on January the 12th 1405. In the preface, our leader is named *"The most excellent and most favourable Lord Owain, Prince of Wales"*. In 1404, he took possession of Aberystwyth and Harlech castles, but Aberystwyth castle was taken back by the King.
After this, as our hero entered Trefaldwyn County (Montgomeryshire), he unexpectedly met a strong army of

---

* Esgair, Pantperthog, Nr Machynlleth (NIDF)
† Lewis's Topographical Dictionary of Wales

Englishmen, on Cwm-du mountain, under the leadership of Earl Warwick; they killed many of his men, and he had to withdraw. But soon after this he assembled a host of men, followed and caught them, giving them a severe 'beating' at Craig y Dorth, near Monmouth. It was Ellis ab Rhisiart ab Hywel ab Morgan Llwyd, from Alrhey, of the lineage of Rhiwallon ab Dyngad ab Tudur Trefor, who now stole Owain's standard. But the Prince had by now passed the pinnacle of his glory, and failure frowned in his face at every step from here on. He was defeated in several battles, and his son, Gruffydd, and his brother, Tudur, were taken prisoner.

The tale was scattered through every corner of Wales that Owain himself had been killed in one of the battles, convincing many of his friends to wane under the command of the King. Friends are often very similar to the shadow; when the sun shines our shadow is obvious at our side, but when it goes under a cloud, there is no more a shadow.

So Owain had to wander from place to place, and from cave to cave, suffering galling adversity. He was, for a period, in a place by the seaside, in the parish of Celynin, around a mile from the River Dysynwy, under the sanctuary of Edfyned ab Aaron, a noble from that neighbourhood of the family of Ednowain ab Bradwen, and this place is called to this day "Ogof Owain" (*"Owain's Cave"*). While here, he was informed that an auxiliary of twelve-thousand soldiers from France, in 140 vessels, had landed in Fishguard.

Owain came out again, and assembled ten-thousand men, who joined the French in Tenby. Having made a number of attacks on the English in the south, the French returned, and the Welsh dispersed. A return French army was sent, but was scattered by tempests while at sea.

Owain continued to keep up his princely grandeur to the end of his

Top: Royal house and Garsiwn area of Machynlleth.
Bottom: Parliament building, Maengwyn Street

time, while making regular attacks on his enemies, the English. The hopes and fears of our hero were ended on the 20th of September, 1415, in the 61st year of his life. It is said that he died in the house of one of his daughters, but whether it was that of the Scudamores at Monington cannot be decided*.

It is said of him that he was *"In terms of his body, shapely and of a grand and dignified appearance – a thorough master of all the elegance of that age: princely in his morals, and charming, easy and confident in his speech; wise in his counsel, and brave in war"†*.

> *Mil a phedwar cant, nid mwy, - cof ydyw*
>   *Cyfodiad Glyndyfrdwy,*
> *A phymptheg praff ei safwy*
> *Bu Owain hen byw yn hwy*

> *No longer than the year fourteen hundred, – this is the memory*
>   *Of the rise of Glyndyfrdwy,*
> *And fifteen, stout was his spear,*
> *Did old Owain live.²*

At the time of the civil war, during the reign of Charles I, Machynlleth suffered a great deal from the campaigns of the terrorists. In January 1644 a host of Sir W. Middleton's men came to the area, harmed two men from Pennal, and then went to Aberystwyth. Again, in November, a great host of his men went to the County of Maesyfed (Radnor) and took as prey many cattle.

---

* In November 1999, the Scudamore family of Monington Court Farm, Golden Valley, near Hay-on-Wye, revealed the suspected location of Glyndwr's grave (NIDF)

† Darlithiau ar Hanes y Cymry, 258

From there he came to Ceredigion, and in Llanbedr (Lampeter) met with 500 Penfro county (Pembrokeshire) men, led by Colonel Ball. They then went on through Llanbadarn until they came close to Machynlleth, where they were met by the commander Hookes and Sir Richard Price, along with men from Meirionnydd (Merionethshire); but Hookes and Price had to retreat through the town until they came to Dyfi Bridge, from where the enemy was kept at bay while reserves and medical supplies lasted. They then retreated again, leaving behind them a number of wounded and one killed. The English then ransacked Machynlleth mercilessly, setting fire to it, before going on to Mathafarn, where they pillaged the place and killed. They then went on through Llanbrynmair to Drefnewydd (Newtown).

A little away from the town, on the main road that leads to Llanidloes, there is a narrow place with two small banks rising each side of it, and this is commonly called *"Carreg-Fasnach"* (*"Trade Rock"*). Machynlleth was visited by the terrible diseases yellow fever and the pox, and the inhabitants of the countryside dreaded going into the town. They therefore held their markets and fairs at this place, from whence it gets its name. At this time they would accept their barter money from buyers in cups of water, and not wash it, as tradition says, in Nant yr Arian (the stream of the silver/money).

Around this place is the expansive Park associated with the town. It is generally reckoned that this was Owain Glyndwr's Park. It is also said that Penyrallt was his rabbit warren. In a *cywydd* poem to him it is recorded that Brynglas, near this town, was his summerhouse.

Puw of Mathafarn once took possession of this Park; he tilled the land, burnt the turfs, planted rye, and hedged around it – the old hedgerows are apparent to this day – and he let it grow high. But the *"Children of the Garsiwn"* stood rigidly by their rights, and one day a host of the townsfolk went up and pulled down the hedges, taking them home to burn; they also let lose the sheep, pigs, and mules to make the most of it, and no one again dared lay a hedge there.

On the plain of the park they used to hold races, and the remains of the courses can still be seen. This is how Mr Pugh, of Tygwyn, near Machynlleth, describes the way in which the races ended:

> "After the Wesleyans came to the town to preach, they and other denominations started warning their people not to go up to the Park to watch the races; and some of them kept medicines in their houses of worship. Some were seen going to the chapel, and some to the park. But that was a means to convince the gentlemen so much, that they gave up the habit completely. There are still some alive in the town that I saw in the chapel listening during the times of the races, around 1803 and 1804."

Some of the local militia of Trefaldwyn county (Montgomeryshire) also used to train here at the time of King George III, and their billet is still on Maengwyn Street to this day; it is there that the majority of the town's weavers work*.

With these few historical facts associated with Machynlleth, we shall remark a little more particularly on its current situation. We cannot say when the name Machynlleth was adopted; and many interpretations and connections have been made in relation to the original name. Some insist that it comes from the legend of the neighbour who shouted to another neighbour *"mae'r moch-yn-y-llaeth"* (*"the pigs are in the milk"*), but it is apparent that this is just

---

* This building, now in ruins and partially demolished, is called the *Barracs* and is near the White Horse Hotel on Maengwyn Street (NIDF)

unfounded bunkum. Others assert that it derives from Cynllaith, a name associated with Owain Glyndwr, because he was known as the Lord of Cynllaith, which is mostly in the parish of Llansilin, and as a consequence that the meaning is *mach,* or the abode of the Lord of *Cynllaith.* But the most commonly held opinion, and most similar to the truth, is that the meaning is Mach-cyn-llaith*, or the creek before the moist place. Whatever is said about this meaning, it appears remarkably natural.

As we take our place on the road that leads to Pennal, at "Bwlch Pennal" the flat and broad vale of the Dyfi stretches ahead, and the town appears to lurk between two small hills, while stretching its head to get a glance of the plains below, which are sometimes flooded by the Dyfi. As we look from a place called Cae-ty'rbugail, near the town, to a point opposite the place called Nawlyn, the same property is apparent.

It is generally accepted by travellers and visitors that, when compared with most of the towns of the Principality, it excels in terms of neatness, organisation, and cleanliness. It is divided into three main streets; namely Maengwyn (Whitestone), which derives its name from a stone, or "maen", of this colour, on the side of the town close to its upper end; Pentrerhedyn; and Penyrallt, which was previously called "The street of the men of Gwynedd"; along with numerous other narrow parts, such as the Garsiwn, the Tol, Graigfach, Maesglas, etc. Its streets are narrow and cleanly, and the houses are mostly of recent construction. Because its position is so convenient, being in a narrow place between the river confluences and the "heartland", and on the border of South and North Wales, and because it enjoys such advantages as a fishing station, a broad range of commerce is carried out here.

Through it alone the riches of the westerly part of the county are

---

*Cathrall's History of North Wales; Cambrian Quarterly Magazine, Vol. I., page 448

transported to reach the sea, including slates, minerals, wood, bark, etc., to send to different areas of the world. Lime, coal, iron, and most domestic materials are also taken through it to reach the surrounding countryside. A market is held in Machynlleth every Wednesday, and it has held this right since early times.

After Gruffydd ap Meredith, the Lord of Powys, submitted to King Henry I, and having given his heirdoms under the patronage of the King to hold as the Marcher Lordships, and to fulfil to the King such service, he was made Lord of Powys, and a Baron of England's Parliament. But after the male offspring of this unscrupulous Welshman faltered, his lands were possessed by his daughter, who, it is said, came under the guardianship of King Edward II, who gave her in marriage to the brave Knight Sir John Charlton. Sir John proved himself to be a good friend to Powys, and was given permission by the King, to whom he was a chamberlain, to hold a market every week in Trallwm (Welshpool) and Machynlleth, as well as two annual fairs in these places.

Popular fairs are also held in Machynlleth on the following days of every year: Wednesday the 1st of March, the Monday before the third Thursday in April, May the 5th (sheep fair), May the 16th, June the 26th, July the 9th, September the 18th and 25th (sheep fair), October the 21st and 26th (sheep fair), November the 26th. A big market is also held on the Wednesday before Easter.

These fairs are amongst the principal markets in Wales in terms of stock and buyers. In the town there are also a host of beautiful and convenient shops, and they certainly have the goods – the food and clothes that can be obtained in them are splendid, and at reasonable prices such as are not to be found in any part of the Kingdom, considering their distance from the places where such things are made.

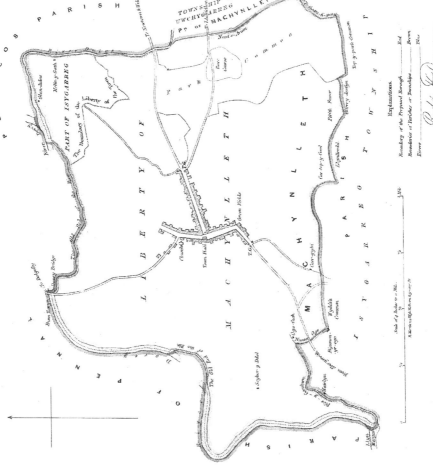

MACHYNLLETH.

Robert Dawson
Lieut R.E.

Explanations.

Boundary of the Proposed Borough .... Red
Boundaries of Parishes or Townships .... Brown
Rivers .... Blue

Map of the Town and Liberty of Machynlleth, produced by Robert K Dawson in the early 1830s as part of a *Report on the Town of Machynlleth,* proposing that it be made contributory to Montgomery.

The map clearly shows the racecourse, close to Nant-yr-Arian, on Parc Common, and a *'small detached portion of the Township of Isygarreg, which adjoins the Township of Machynlleth on the North-east'.*

The report recommended that *'the future Borough of Machynlleth shall comprise the whole of the Township and Liberty of Machynlleth, and the portion of Isygarreg Township before-mentioned'*

28

Machynlleth's main industry is wool processing; its whole surroundings are chequered with mills, wool factories, fulling mills, etc., but there are not as many of them in the town as is often seen in other places, and this adds a great deal to its beauty and wholesomeness.

The inhabitants benefit from plentiful clean water poured from pumping machines, in addition to numerous springs and wells, such as Pistill Gwyn, on the slope of Penrallt hill, and Ffynnon y Garsiwn, in the part of the town so named, which is notable for its strong spring, and crystal clear pure water.

It can be said that our town is capable of providing comfortable and entertaining accommodation for visitors, and every necessary facility for travellers and others. There are a host of reputable houses for accommodation, in addition to numerous inns, and ample and beautiful, very clean and organised hotels; but that which is considered to be at the top of the list is the Wynnstay Arms Hotel*, which is kept by Mr C. J. Lloyd. The Herbert Arms†, kept by Mr D. Jones, also wins high praise. In these places there are a wide variety of carriages and horses always ready to hire, and the compliments strangers pay to these places is assurance enough of their excellence, and the favourability of their charges. Numerous other small places are clean and comfortable.

The mail coach runs through the town daily from Amwythig (Shrewsbury), through Trallwm (Welshpool), Drefnewydd (Newtown), Carno, and Llanbrynmair, to Aberystwyth, at 11.30 in the morning; and from Aberystwyth to Amwythig (Shrewsbury) along the same route at 1.52 in the afternoon. The carriage "Engineer" runs four fast horses through the town daily during the summer, and every other day during other seasons, from

---

* The Wynnstay referred to is now a newsagents, behind town clock.
† The Herbert Arms referred to is now called the Wynnstay Hotel

29

Aberystwyth to Croesoswallt (Oswestry) at 9.30 in the morning, through Mallwyd, Cann-Office, Meifod, etc., to meet the carriage to Llynlleifiaid (Liverpool), Manceinion (Manchester), Llundain (London), and every part of the Kingdom; this returns the same way at 5.30 in the afternoon. Some other carriages normally run through the town during the summer, to Dolgellau, Tan y Bwlch (Maentwrog), Beddgelert, and Caernarfon; and to Aberdyfi and Tywyn. It is not behind, either, in terms of facilities to deliver goods and other heavy things from one place to another. Apart from the multitude carried around the town, some also go regularly to Amwythig (Shrewsbury), through Llanbrynmair, Carno, Y Drefnewydd (Newtown), and Trallwm (Welshpool), every Monday, returning on the same road by Saturday; to Y Drefnewydd (Newtown) every Monday and Thursday; to Aberystwyth every Monday; to Dolgellau every Saturday; to Aberdyfi and Tywyn every Wednesday and Saturday; to Merthyr and Tredegar through Llanidloes, Rhaiadr, Builth, etc., every month, on the Tuesday morning before the first Saturday in every month.

The town has recently risen highly in the attentions of the gentry of our country as a fishing station through its proximity to streams and rivers so full of fish, especially trout and salmon, the latter of which is supposed to be among the best in the Kingdom (see DYFI).

The post-house stands by the town hall, in Maengwyn Street. Letters from England are dispached at 12 noon, and are sent forth at 1 in the afternoon. They arrive from Aberystwyth and South Wales at 2, and are sent forth at 11.30 in the morning.

There is a National Provincial Bank of England in Pentrerhedyn Street, which is managed by John Jones Esq. The savings bank is kept on Maengwyn Street: J Jones Esquire, Treasurer, D Howell Esq. secretary. There are also numerous clubs associated with the town which assist their members in cases of illness and failings, including the "Friendly Society", kept in the house of Mrs Ann Morgan. This was established in the year 1834, and its capital is currently more than £700. Its annual distribution is held on Saint David's day – the first of March. The "Benefaction Society" is kept at the Herbert Arms, and holds its distribution annually on the 29th of May. Its capital is currently over £120. The "Clothing Society", set up to assist the poor to buy clothes and other necessary things, is sustained through the underwritings of those gentlemen and ladies of the town and the neighbourhood who pay 2s 6d annually on behalf of each member, in addition to the contribution of a penny a week from members themselves, who now number more than 120. The annual distribution is held on the first day of March, and the manager is Mr Lewis, curate of the parish.

In 1853, an excellent Society was established here, called "The Machynlleth Herbaceous and Horticultural Society", and it is a pleasure to note its progress and success. Its President is Earl Vane, Plâs Machynlleth, and the Vice President is F J Ford Esq., Llwyngwern. Its sponsors are Baroness Vane; Mrs Ford, Llwyngwern; Mrs Ruck, Pantlludw; and Mrs Phelps, Bron y Gog. The Treasurer is Mr John Thomas, pharmacist, and the Secretary Mr W W Jones, solicitor. Prizes are offered for the cleanest and most orderly cottages, the most cultivated gardens, the best plants and fruits, and the most pretty and pleasing vegetables and flowers. Every cottager residing within 10 miles of Machynlleth whose tax is below £4 has the full right to compete for any number of the prizes offered.

During the last year a host of the youth of the town assembled together and formed the "Literary Society". Their meetings are held weekly in the Town Hall, and occasionally competition meetings are held to reward successful candidates in poetry and essays – and this portrait is among the fruits of such prizes. It is pleasing to see the desire and energy demonstrated by the youth to attain knowledge, and to embrace those things which tend to elevate man's position of morality and understanding. But it is regrettable to have to say that it has not so far received the support deserved from the hands of responsible inhabitants and the neighbourhood, and I would use this opportunity to draw their attention to it, for the cause is truly deserving of every support.

In terms of this area, I cannot pass by without alluding to the fact that it is lamentable of our town that there is not within it so much as one Public Library, or lectern, or News Room. If we could get enough support to form these, it is certain to me that it would excite more efforts and vitality – the inhabitants would come to contemplate more on the great subjects of religion and politics, the affairs of the world, and the discussions of different generations would be familiar to them. Information on the arts and daily betterment would be more advertised, which would set them on ground to be able to keep up with the age, and to promote that age to a pinnacle, when the worthiness of the greatest part of a man will be his standard of respect and honour. This would also put an effective curb on the ways of many of badness and wildness in the midst of our youth. It would also teach them to *think* instead of reprobating, and spend their facilities and the advantages of the term of youth to seek beneficial knowledge, for their own sakes, the sake of their age, and their country.

In relation to Machynlleth's civil position, it can be said that it has, like the boroughs of Llanidloes, Y Drefnewydd (Newtown), Llanfyllyn, Y Trallwm (Welshpool), and Trefaldwyn (Montgomery), the right to vote in the election of a Member of Parliament. This privilege was received originally back in the 27th year of Henry VIII, and existed between the years 1536 and 1728, at which time the privilege was withdrawn from all but Trefaldwyn (Montgomery). In the year 1831 the former right was restored, and its voters currently number around 80. It was also made a place to poll electors for a Member of Parliament across the county.

The Petty Courts* for the hundred of Cyfeiliog are held here, and it also forms part of the Circuit of the twenty-nine Courts of petty debtors. These meetings are held, as are most other public meetings, in the Town Hall, which is a simple, strong building, standing in the centre of the town, and without moving from it, it is possible to get a full view of the main streets instantly[†]. Behind it is a designated place to hold the meat market, held on each Wednesday and Saturday. The hall was built in 1783 by Sir Watkin Williams Wynne Bart., who is the Lord of the Manor, and holds a Grand Court once a year. A gaol was built in 1849, which is a strong and smart building, standing on slightly raised land, at the top end of Maengwyn Street, in a wholesome place, and the rooms are kept clean and orderly. The gaol-keeper attests that the crimes are very few, and the punishments administered there are comparable to any other one place in the county, which speaks volumes as to its morality and religiousness. Associated with the town are spacious parks, in the forms of Penyrallt and the Wylfa, onto which places everyone has a right to turn out their livestock without charge.

There are numerous houses of worship in Machynlleth belonging to both the established church and the different religious denominations. The church of the parish stands on Penyrallt Street, and is rather recent, with the exception of the bell-tower, which was built in 1745. Its interior is apportioned well, and is laid out in an orderly way. The old bell tower is erected higher than the rest of the

---

* Magistrates Courts (NIDF)
[†] Machynlleth Town Hall formerly stood at the main junction in the centre of the town. The hall was replaced in 1873 by the Castlereagh Memorial Clock, built to mark the 21st birthday of Viscount Castlereagh.

church, and has angular pinnacles set at its top. The church is dedicated to Saint Peter, and is in the incumbency of Llanelwy, under the patronage of the Bishop of that place. Ieuan Llawdden, a famous bard from the area of Llychwyr in Glamorgan, was a minister in this parish from the year 1430 to 1470, when he returned to his own area of birth to spend his latter days. Hywel Swrdwal, a notable bard of the fifteenth century, was also a clergyman here. The current incumbent is the Reverend George Venables M.A.. The graveyard is flat and orderly, and has recently been enlarged. There are also houses of worship in the town associated with the Calvinistic Methodists, the Independents, the Wesleyans, and the Mormons.

In the year 1829 a National School was established under the patronage of the late John Jones, Esq., of London. Sir Watkin Williams Wynn gave money to construct it, in an agreeable place in Toll Street*, with the expansive flats of the vale of the Dyfi stretching beautifully from its front. The houses of the school are robust and attractive, and are kept clean and tidy. It is honourably sustained through the bequests of £36:16:0 per year from the aforesaid John Jones, Esq.; £6:15:0 from the late John Owen Esq., Llynlloedd; and £2:0:0 from the late Mrs Ann Jones, as well as the generous underwritings of other gentlemen of the neighbourhood. The boys are taught by a schoolmaster, and the girls by a schoolmistress, and they are assisted by numerous undergraduates.

In 1852 the "Vane Infant School" was erected in honour of the birth of the Heir of Plâs Machynlleth for the purpose of instructing small children in the "ends of their ways", and, to this end, just as the arrows are in the hands of the strong, so are the young children. Education in the school is provided by a schoolmistress. A little

---

* *Toll Street* (i.e. street with a toll gate) is the correct translation of *Heol y Doll*, the *T* in *Toll* having mutated to a *D* in the Welsh spelling. However, the street is now known in English as *Doll Street*.(NIDF)

above this place is an old building which is now in ruins, where it is said that the Monks of Machynlleth lived. While digging to make a foundation for the new school a deep hole in the ground was found, around a yard in diameter, but they did not go to the trouble of investigating it.

The main mansions of the Gentry that surround the town are: Plâs Machynlleth, the excellent residence of Earl Vane, the associated gardens of which are full of every variety of agreeable plants and fruits. The avenues are beautiful and wholesome, and the parks and their surroundings are expansive, and mostly flat, being varied by an occasional large tree, and wild goats frolicking along it; Bron-y-gog, the residence of S. Phelps, Esq.; Pen-yr-allt, the residence of H. J. Evans, Esq.; Gallt-y-llan, the residence of F. J. Ford, Esq., and Pantlludw, the residence of Laurence Ruck, Esq.[*]

MACHYNLLETH, THE PARISH

It seems apparent that the name of the parish is derived from the town of the same name. It is understood that it includes around 5000 acres of land, most of it high and mountainous. The highest parts are good grazing for sheep and other animals, and the lowlands are exceptionally fertile and productive. Its population in 1851 was 1663. It includes three tithe-townships: the town itself, Is-y-garreg, and Uwch-y-garreg, and the poor of these townships are supported separately.

In the parish church, in Machynlleth, there is a list of endowments left to the poor of the parish, from which the following translation is provided:-

---

[*] See "A Trickle of Welsh Blood" by Bertha Ruck (NIDF)

BEQUESTS TO THE POOR OF THIS TOWN AND THE PARISH

1. ISAAC PUGH, late of this town, a gentleman who left in his will three houses for the poor of the town, for ever, to be let by the parson and churchwardens of the church of this Parish, and their successors, for ever, and to share the rent on Christmas night.

2. DAVID PARRY, from the Kingdom of Ireland, Esquire, who left in his will fifty-five pounds to the poor of this Parish; the interest of which is to be shared annually by the parson and churchwardens of the church on St Andrew's day.

3. ROWLAND OWEN, from Llynlloedd, Esquire, who left in his will the interest on forty pounds to the poor of this town and the Parish, to be shared annually by the parson and churchwardens of the church on St Andrew's day for ever.

4. GWEN OWEN, late of this Parish, a widowed woman, who left in her will the interest on twenty-five pounds to the poor of this parish, to be shared annually on St Andrew's day, for ever.

5. JOHN DAVIES, late of this town, a gentleman who left in his final will twenty pounds, to be shared annually on Christmas night, for ever.

6. LEWIS HUMPHREYS, late of this Parish, a gentleman who left in his final will the annual interest on twenty pounds towards apprenticing any poor boy or girl from this town.

7. HUMPHREY MORRIS, late of this town, a gentleman who left in his final will all of the new houses recently erected between the houses of Edward Lewis and Thomas Pugh, gentlemen, as a dwelling place for the poor and deprived from this town, and the interest on sixty pounds, for ever, to the following dependents:- ten shillings towards repairing the aforesaid houses, and to provide bed-clothes for such deprived families; thirty shillings towards giving daily schooling to six poor boys or girls from this town; and twenty shillings towards apprenticing any poor child from the aforesaid town.

8. JOHN OWEN, from Llynlloedd, Esquire, who left in his last will the annual interest on two-hundred pounds towards supporting the free school of this town.

MACHYNLLETH, UNION

The Union of Machynlleth includes the Parishes and tithe-townships of Machynlleth, Tywyn, Pennal, Llanbrynmair, Llanwrin, Penegoes, Cemmaes, Darowen, Scubor-y-coed, Uwch-y-garreg, and Is-y-garreg. The Overseers of the poor in these parishes assemble together in the Board Room, in Maengwyn Street, Machynlleth, every second Wednesday. Chairman; H. J. Evans, Esq., Penyrallt. Secretary: D. Howell, Esq., lawyer.

ABERDYFI

A harbour and bathing place in the Parish of Tywyn, in the hundred of Ystumaner, Meirionnydd (Merionethshire), 4 miles to the southeast of the town of Tywyn, and 10 miles to the west of Machynlleth.

The position of the village is agreeable; it is on the northern side of the River Dyfi, where the river discharges into the sea, from which it gets its name*. Behind it rises a hill, from which protrude two outcrops, like two limbs hugging the village in their warm embrace.

There are a great number of houses here, and they are almost all beautiful new buildings. In the row that faces the sea, in particular, can be found houses that hold their place in parallel with the most splendid ones in Marine Terrace, Aberystwyth.

The larger part of the village is made up of a place called Penhelyg, which, in a way, forms a small harbour on its own, to its east. The majority of ships are built here, and the small pretty mansion of the patriotic Welshman and antiquarian J. Pughe Esq., F.R.C.S. (Ioan ab Huw, Doctor) is also here. A small new schoolhouse has recently been built on the high place near the road between Penhelyg and the village.

There are five religious denominations here. The Established Church, which is a small, very magnificent building, and an adornment to the village, was gifted with a clock and colourful window by R. Scott Esq. It is dedicated to St Peter. The Wesleyans, Calvinistic Methodists, Independents, and Brethren have houses of worship here. The Post Office is kept in the market-house of Mr R. Edwards.

Aberdyfi is frequented by large hordes of respectable visitors. Comfortable lodgings for families can be found here; the *Corbet Arms Hotel,* which is a little to the west of the village, is a spacious and convenient place, which is kept clean and tidy. It has recently attracted significant attention as a suitable winter residence for the

---

* Aber = an estuary or the mouth of a river

clergy. The breeze is mild and pleasing, and the weather usually agreeable and wholesome. The beach is magnificent, and composed of hard sand, such that a carriage can travel safely on it for about six miles. It is covered by a large variety of shells.

Aberdyfi was once a main harbour for Ceredigion (Cardiganshire), and the main toll-house was kept here, rather than in Aberystwyth as it is at present. The illustrious bard and litterateur *Llewelyn Ddu o Fôn,* patron of the genius Gorony Owen, and the learned Ieuan Brydydd Hir, collected taxes here for a long period[*].

The estuary is considered to be one of the best harbours in the Principality, and ships of the largest size can enter it and float at anchor with the greatest safety. Perhaps it is this estuary that the triad referred to when it was said *"The three privileged harbours of Britain: Ysgewin port in Gwent, Wygyr in Mon (Anglesey), and Wyddnaw in Ceredigion (Cardiganshire)".* The commerce is extensive in terms of sending bark, slates, wood, minerals, etc., to every part of the Principality, and even to foreign countries; limestone, earthenware, coal, and other things of domestic use are also imported through here.

It appears from history that industry has continued in Aberdyfi since somewhat early times. It is reported to us in the chronicles that Cadwgan ab Bleddyn ab Cynfyn, Prince of Powys, held an honorary feast for the noblemen of the nation in Aberteifi (Cardigan) Castle, inviting the best bards and musicians in all Wales, and that after finishing the feast, everyone returned home burdened with generous gifts.

During the feast it happened that, for the worse, Owain ab Cadwgan fell in love with Nest, the daughter of Rhys ab Tewdwr, who was the wife of Gerallt, the keeper of Pembroke Castle. To complete his terrible intention Owain, accompanied by a few friends, went to see

---

[*] Gwladgarwr, vol. vi, page 98

Nest; for Bleddyn, Owain's father, and Gwladus, Nest's mother, were cousins. Sometime in the still of the night, having succeeded in getting in, Owain set the room where Gerallt and Nest were sleeping on fire. The two woke up in the greatest inferno, and before long Nest realised the betrayal, and helped Gerallt to escape. Then Owain took Nest and her two sons, and stole them away to Powys.

Despite all the orders of King Henry, Cadwgan and Owain would not give the woman back to Gerallt. Because of this, Ithel and Madawe, the sons of Ririt and Llywarch ab Trahearn, and Uchdrud son of Edwin were incensed to take revenge for this injustice on Owain; they assembled their hosts, and spoiled the lands of the offenders; but Cadwgan and Owain succeeded in escaping in a ship from Aberdyfi to Ireland, where they remained for a year before returning.

According to some lines written by two brothers, John and Richard Philip, from Hendrefechan, in Ardudwy, a Spanish ship appeared entering Aberdyfi harbour in 1597, with the intention of landing a few men for the purpose of pillaging the inhabitants. The bards suggest that it was one of the escaped *Spanish Armada,* from 1588, and it seems likely that this took place, because before landing, the wind pushed it back out to sea.

Because this place stands at the periphery of the North and South, it appears that it suffered severely many times from the campaigns of the Princes of the surrounding provinces to invade each others rights and territories.

Around the year 1135, the wrath of Cadwaladr and Owain, the sons of Gruffydd ab Cynan, Prince of Gwynedd, was inflamed against the foreigners who set themselves up in Ceredigion (Cardiganshire), and they came with the whole elite of their country with the intention of completely destroying them. They decimated the castles of Gwallter, Aberystwyth, Dinerth, and Caer Wedros, and then returned to the north. However, at the end of that year they came to Ceredigion (Cardiganshire) for a second time, and with them were about six-thousand selected fighters from Gwynedd. Hywel ab Meredydd from Brycheiniog (Breconshire) also came and aided them. These all assembled their armies in Aberdyfi. To face them came Robert son of Martin, and the sons of Gerallt Ystiwart, and all the Flemish, and the whole arms of France. Having fought long and hard on each side, the Normans and the Flemish fled. They were pursued by the Welsh, and a great number of them were killed. Others were burned, their horses spoiled, and many others were taken prisoner, while most were drowned like fools in the river. Having lost around three-thousand men they departed the land, after which Owain and Cadwaladr returned, having had complete victory, and valuable prey.

In the year 1151, the Lord Rhys, Prince of the South, sent an envoy to all the Princes and aristocrats of our country, to ask for their support in sending away the French and the English from all of Wales. But he did not have his request grated. In this patriotic attempt to form a powerful Welsh council to defeat their enemies, there was not one request sent by Rhys to Owain Gwynedd for support; and the reason for this, it seems, is that there was some crucially malicious jealousy between the two Princes; for a little after this we read that Rhys heard that Owain was bringing a large host to Ceredigion (Cardiganshire), and on hearing this he assembled a host, and came to Aberdyfi to meet him with the capability of defeating him. Before long Rhys built a castle here, in a place currently called Bryncelwydd, and he returned to the South.

It is indisputable that "Dyfi Castle" suffered a great deal in its time from enemy attacks. It is shown that it was completely destroyed around 1157 by Robert, Earl Clare, one of the Marcher Lords, such that there are now no remains of it to be seen.

In the year 1215, when excitement surrounded the Magna Carta, for the purpose of the Welsh repossessing the lands stolen from them by the Marcher Lords, and to enjoy from then on the same rights as the English, they joined the English Lords to exact their rights from King John.

> *"During this time there was revealed, in the midst of the Welsh, a notable and praiseworthy tendency to cooperate in order to maintain national unity and peace between themselves,; and for the purpose of training their intentions a council was held in Aberdyfi, to which came Llewelyn ab Iorwerth, and all the Princes of Wales, along with all the wise men of Gwynedd; and before the Prince the territories of the south were shared among the candidates in the south"**.

After the King had made several forays along the borders of Wales, he returned to England, where he died soon afterwards, and through this the privileged candidates secured the Magna Carta.

In this village there once lived the famous bard Ieuan Dyfi. We do not have any clear history of this Welshman, but it is said by credible authorities that he was the oldest son of Dafydd, the brother of Llewelyn ab Griffydd, and that he went with King John to France, when the battle of Pointers was fought. He had, under his authority, around 300 Welshmen. After this, Ieuan went to Lombardy. But when the war broke out again in 1369 he returned to France, and put his sword under the authority of King Charles. Michelet said of him that *"One of the best commanders who served France is a Welshman, descended from the old Princes of Wales"*. King Charles cherished such an opinion of Ieuan that he offered to

---

* Hanes Cymru by Carnhuanawc, 635

aid him with 300,000 gold francs, for the purpose of repossessing his heirdom. In 1372 Ieuan came with four thousand soldiers from France, and attacked the island of Guernsey, which he took. In the meantime, the English also suffered a large loss in a war against the Spanish navy, which took Earl Pembroke and many other officers prisoner.

The King of France encouraged Ieuan to go to Spain to try and secure support from its King, and this he obeyed. But funnily enough he happened to land in St Andero on the same day as the Earl of Pembroke came in with his countrymen. They met each other in a hostel there. Ieuan, being short-tempered, addressed the captured gentleman as follows: *"Earl Pembroke, did you come here to pay homage to me for the land that you hold on my behalf in the Principality of Wales, the place that your King deprived me of upon the counsel of evil men?"* "Who are you who addresses me with such words?" replied the surprised Earl

"I am Ieuan, the son and heir of the Prince of Wales, he who wickedly put your King to death, and for the dispossession of my lands; but perhaps I can, through the aid of my lord, the King of France, adopt a remedy for this, and I will surely do this. I wish to make you aware that, if I can meet you in an appropriate place, I will surely fight you. I will show you the injustice you, as well as the Earl Henffordd (Hereford) and Edward Spencer, did to me, because through your father, and other evil counsellors, you betrayed my lord and my father, which should anger me, and I will take revenge for this whenever I get the opportunity". Sir Thomas St Aubyn, a comrade of Earl Pembroke said *"Ieuan; if you say to my lord now, or at any time, that you will commit any disrespectful act, or cease to my lord to undo, or if he has any cause to submit to you, throw your glove to the floor, and here is one ready to take it up".* "You are a prisoner" said Ieuan. *"I would not win any honour through calling you out, since you are not on*

your own property, but on that of those who took you; but when you get your freedom I shall speak to you more boldly, since things cannot stay as they are".

But in 1378, Ieuan accepted an order from the brother of the King of France to go and attack Mortain-sur-Mer. While holding this castle under siege, Ieuan fell to clandestine murder by John Lanbe, who had become a bosom friend of his. *"So"* said one *"Ieuan of Wales fell to the great sorrow of the King and the people. Charles grieved a great deal but could not undo his fate. Ieuan was buried in the castle of St Leger, with great grandeur and honour"*. This, it seems, was the course and fate of our countryman, who was known to us better by the name Ieuan Dyfi.

It was no small advantage that Aberdyfi won through the establishment, in 1827, of a main road which leads from Pennal to Tywyn. This runs to the north of the River Dyfi, through expansive and majestic scenery. From one side can be seen Ceredigion (Cardiganshire) stretching away, and the silvery beach of the river dispersed in front of us; and from parts of it can be had a glimpse of the main mountains of North Wales venturing towards the heavens. It is mostly cut through hard rock; and the different risings of the hills, and the myriad vegetation and plants which adorn them, countless in their beauties, make it a truly pleasant and beautiful drive.

On our journey along it we get a view of cleanly farms and cultivated land, and the mansions of the following gentlemen: Talgarth, being hidden almost entirely by thick-crested trees, the residence of C. F. Thruston Esq.; the new mansion recently erected by C. T. Thruston Esq., with its elevated tower, sitting like a monarch in the midst of

---

* Froissart, book i. chapter cccvii

44

open expansive land*; Penmaen Dyfi, lurking in the shadow of the woods, the residence of John Vaughan Esq.; Gogarth, the residence of the Rev. L Hughes; Trefri, or Tref-rydd, or a name that would be much more appropriate for it, "Craig-y-Don", which sits between the rocks as if to wash its feet in the river, the home of R D Jones Esq., the owner of Aberllefenny slate quarries. The learned Dr. John Pugh, Aberdyfi, said that a terrible marauder lived in Trefrydd during the reign of Henry IV, but the hero, Jenkin Vaughan from Gaethle, sent him off. Also, Braich-y-celyn, residence of the Rev. J Griffiths, Vicar of Aberdar.

During the making of the aforementioned road, a vessel was found next to Braich-y-celyn containing numerous pieces of early English-minted coins, and, in 1824, in the sand on the beach, a Tuscan decorated earthenware vase was found, capable of holding around two quarts†, which is now in the possession of the Rev. Isaac Bonsal, Llanwrin.

ABERANGELL

A row of houses on the side of the road that leads from Llanwrin to Mallwyd, around 10½ miles to the northwest of Machynlleth. The village is positioned to the north of the River Dyfi, on the side of a small stream called the Angell, which discharges into the Dyfi, giving it its name. Most of the inhabitants are poor labourers. One of the most excellent watermills in Wales is located here, built by J W. Astley Esq., Cwmllecoediog. Most of the inhabitants are Calvinistic Methodists for whom there is a house of worship here.

The area is pleasant and fruitful, and is irrigated by the two aforementioned rivers. Around a mile above the village, in the

---

* Trefanau, known as Pennal Towers
† A quart is two pints; i.e. a quarter of a gallon

middle of enclosed beech woods, stands the mansion of Cwmllecoediog (Valley of the wooded place) – the name of which is truly literal. This was built by J. W. Astley Esq., and the family lived here for a long period, but have left the area many years since. The late inhabitant, Henry Foskett Esq., made considerable improvements there, and amongst other things made an extensive fish lake near the house. It is said that a copper mine was discovered in a place nearby.

ABERFFRWDLAN

This farmhouse stands in the shade of beech trees, by the side of the road that leads from Machynlleth to Llanwrin. The name signifies *'the discharge of a sparkling stream into the river'*. It was here that the late Lady Peniarth resided, and what remains of the old mansion is evidence enough of its original magnificence. Tradition says that the excellent furnishings that were there at the time of the Lady were buried in a meadow between it and the River Dyfi, and no one dared search for them.

A little away from the farmhouse is a slight rise of land called "Rhiw'r cyrff", and in the "prophecy" of Myrddin there are a few lines thought to refer to it. They are as follows:

> *Ceir gwel'd ymladdfa greulon*
> *Ar gefn cethin fryn;*
> *A'r gwaed a fydd yn llifo*
> *Ar hyd gleddyfau'n llyn:*
> *Y cyrn a fydd yn canu*
> *Oddeutu Abernant;*
> *Ac ar Riw'r cyrff ond odid*
> *Y lleddir llawer cant.*

There will be a cruel battle
  On the side of a dark hill,
And there the blood will flow
  As liquid on the swords:
The horns will be a-blowing
  About all Abernant;
And on Rhiw'r cyrff (the hill of the corpses), perhaps,
  Many hundreds will be slain.²

I heard some saying that their grandfathers told them that they had seen many old war weapons dug out of the earth in these surroundings.

ABERGANOLWYN

A small country village in the parish of Llanfihangel-y-Pennant, in the midst of the mountains, around 12 miles from Machynlleth, on the road that leads from Talyllyn to Tywyn. There is a hotel here, and a house of worship owned by the Wesleyans.

ABERHOSAN

After travelling around 4 miles along the main road that leads from Machynlleth to Llanidloes, we turn onto a track on our right, and wander ahead for around a mile without meeting anything to particularly attract our attention except the peaked mountains that rise in front of us, as if to bar our destination, when suddenly, a few grey, poorly to look at, houses come into view, set back against the sides of the hills – this is Aberhosan. It is situated on the banks of a small river called the Carog. In relation to the meaning of the name, it is unknown.

There is a robust and convenient house of worship owned by the Independents located here. It is reported that during the early religious revival in Wales, the Calvinistic Methodists came here to preach, and that the Missionaries suffered bitter persecution. One time a gentleman by the name of Mr Llwyd came to preach here, as well as a greater body of men than usual. However, after the service had begun a young man in the congregation stood up and said he wished him to be silent, and started to move forward towards the speaker and the pulpit. Some in the congregation said to him *"Oh Deio don't, all he wants is to do good to you and all of us"*. But he took no notice of this and pushed forward with all his might. Mr Llwyd, seeing this, said *"Take it quietly brothers, let him come here to me, I am certain that I have greater excellence in the matter that he is following, greater than he has achieved to date."*

When Deio heard this he soon stood still, and no one dared further disturb the preacher.

There is a blooming Literary Society here, under the patronage and presidency of the patriotic and cordial litterateur Edward Davies Esq., Dolcaradog. It does not appear that any industry is carried out in the village, and the residents are sustained through working on the surrounding farms. Although most of the area is mountainous and high, and the land is not the most fertile, the hands of the diligent farmers keep its appearance organised, and while taking note of the land, some charming satisfaction is felt.

Because this place is at the foot of the high mountain of Pumlimmon, and so close to those places which are the sites of many bloody battles, it is beyond question that the area did not escape without being tarnished by human blood, as proved by the names of the farms close-by, such as Braich-Ithel-gam, Dolcaradog, etc., as well as the tradition that exists among the inhabitants.

On the edge of the road, a little lower down than the place where we turn towards the village*, there is the farmhouse of Croeslyn, or "lun croes" (image of a cross), which, it is presumed, gave its name to the parish of Penegoes, or Pen-y-groes. Close to it stands a strong, broad-girthed yew, and it is likely that it stands there to mark the quiet place of rest of a host of our fellow men, those perhaps who fell in the bloody wars that took place here. Also in the area is a farmhouse called Mynachdy, and I heard one old man who had lived there for a long time saying that odd pieces of the walls of the old monastery could be seen when he was a youth; and perhaps Croeslyn was also related to such folk[†].

ABERLLEFENNY –See CORRIS

ABERCEGIR

A large-breadthed village in the parish of Darowen, 5 miles from Machynlleth. The name signifies *'the discharge or estuary of the small River Cegir'* into the Gwidol. The village stands prettily on the

---

* Croeslyn is above where the modern road turns for Aberhosan (NIDF)

[†] During the late 12th Century, Owain Cyfeiliog's son, Gwenwynwyn, gave lands in the Uwchygarreg and Aberhosan area to the Cistercian monks of Ystrad Marchell (Strata Marcella), his father having previously helped to establish that monastery by granting land in the Welshpool area to the Abbot of Hendy-gwyn (Whitland). The land included large tracts of the northern Plunlumon range, stretching from Glaslyn to Nant y Moch, as well as an area referred to as Pennant Cynlling, which included Hengwm (old valley) and Mynachdy (Monks house).

*Capel Bethlehem, Aberhosan, viewed from the slopes of Foel
Fadian, with Machynlleth and Taran Hendre in the distance.*

slope of a hill, with the River Gwidol flowing underneath it, and
another small hill ascending opposite, on the other side of the river.
The main road from Machynlleth to Bont-dolgadfan runs through it.
Somewhat extensive industry is carried out here in terms of treating
wool, and the village contains a host of weavers, woollen factories,
and fulling mills. There is a house of worship belonging to the
Wesleyans here.

ABERGWYDOL –See GWYDOL

ARAN-Y-GESAIL*

A mountain in the hundred of Ysumaner, whose height is 2224 feet above the surface of the sea.

BLAENGESYRCH

A Tithe-township in the parish of Llanwrin, around 6 miles from Machynlleth. It is named after the small brook by the name of Glosyrch which runs through it. The land is somewhat high and severe, but splendid views can be seen from some of the tall cliffs of a number of the high mountains of North Wales, and the beautiful valley of the Dyfi and that crystal river meandering through it. It is said that it is extraordinary for its large variety of wild birds, but especially the woodcock.

BLAEN-Y-PANT

As the words signify[†], this village stands at the head of a small dingle in the parish of Machynlleth, around 4 miles from that town. There is a chapel owned by the Wesleyans here.

BUGEILYN

Having travelled uphill for around 8 miles along the road that leads from Machynlleth to Llanidloes, one of the most lonely and wild roads in the Principality, we leave it and take the path on our

---

* Taran y Gesail
† Blaen-y-Pant = Head of the Hollow

southern side, wandering along the tracks of the trolleys that carry the peat from the mountain, for around 2 or 3 miles. Having put our animals in the convenient stable that has been erected by the lake, we start towards it. Here is Bugeilyn stretching in front of us, and, such as we can judge with our eyes, we presume it is around three quarters of a mile in length, and around 300 yards in width. The trout in it are pretty to look at and of considerable size. It is kept consistent under careful management, and, before having the freedom to fish in it, a ticket must be obtained; these can be obtained from J. O. Jones Esq., Dolycorsllwyn, near Cemmaes, or from Mr C. J. Lloyd, Wynnstay Arms, Machynlleth.

In relation to the fact that there were initially no fish in the lake, and the way whereby they came to be there, one author writes as follows[*]: -

> "The circumstances associated with Bugeilyn are against the normal laws of nature: twenty years ago (1829) there were no fish there. Around this time while some gentlemen were hunting grouse on Pumlimmon, their conversation turned to the peculiar fact that that Bugeilyn was devoid of the finned clan, and the possibility of satisfying this with some from a neighbouring stream: they exacted a net, and caught a few dozen trout in the River Rheidol, and transferred them to the lake. At that time a myriad of horse leeches thrived there.
>
> "When some of the fish were placed in the lake, they lay on their sides, weak and fainting. But as was strangely shown, the predatory leeches attached themselves to the weak fish, and totally destroyed them. Other fishes demonstrated

---

[*] Cambrian Quarterly Magazine, vol. i. page 447

themselves to be more manly: those that caught the lex talionis* and took revenge, and made them recede, such as there is not as much as one leech to see at present. The late Gadben Jones R.N., from Machynlleth, and other gentlemen who are still alive were the persons alluded to above.

"In relation to this we ask why this peculiarity is related to the nature of Bugeilyn? I sought all information on the matter, and after some labour, and a great deal of research, I am venturing to offer my own observations on the matter, in relation to the absence of fish previous to this, and their fast multiplication thereafter.

"It is widely known that a mineral mixture is harmful to fish, and it is undisputable that the extensive mine workings that are around it fill it with poisonous substances, and it is likely that a share of the mineral is currently layered on the bottom. Yet by what means are fish living and thriving there now? Between the lake and the peat-land on the western side, a ridge of rocky lamina mantle runs like a dam between the lake and the soft broken layers that are also to be found on the opposite sides. The waters, through being forced by the easterly storms with an indescribable flow, eventually break through this mantle of lime, and as a result a great deal of peaty ground is dispersed, such that a thick layer of black earth is diffused over its whole bottom, except on the westerly side which is quite safe as it is sheltered by a deposit of gravel, which is as hard as the floor of a malthouse.

---

* Lex talionis = law of retribution

"This is confirmed beyond doubt, as every yard of the lake has been investigated with the help of a coracle. It is likely that these layers neutralised the effect of the poison, or at least prevented it transferring to the lake any destructive effect."

CEMMAES

A parish in the hundred of Cyfeiliog, with its position on the southeast of the River Dyfi. The meaning of the word is arena (*Amphitheatre*), or playing field*, and many of the circles where games took place can still be found, here and there, the length of the parish.

It is around 8 miles in length, from the bank of the River Twymyn, at the lower end, to the foot of Bwlch-y-fedwen at the top end, and a mile and a half on average in width. It includes the tithe-townships of Brynuchel, Gwern-y-bwlch, and Tafolog. Its population in 1851 was 891. Around two parts in three are sheep-walks belonging to the owners of the lands that are there.

A number of bequests were left by generous philanthropists to be distributed amongst the poor of this parish; one by Derwas Griffith in 1669, who left a smallholding in the parish of Llanbrynmair, towards the service of this parish and Darowen. The annual rent of the smallholding is £7, which is shared by the incumbent of Cemmaes between the overseers of the two parishes who, at around Christmas time, indiscriminately distribute any monies amongst the poor in small rations of 6 pence, up to 2 shillings each.

---

* Gêm-maes = game-field (NIDF)

*The Dyfi Valley, looking over the village of Cemmaes
towards Aran Fawddwy.*

The two parishes jointly contribute towards repairing the buildings on the aforementioned smallholding; also, the sum of £40 by Mrs. Bridget Mostyn, given in 1730, and £20 given by Grace Pryce in 1784, and the rent, namely 20 shillings, which is derived from a smallholding in this parish called Cegidog Fawr.

At the lower end of this parish there is a very broad village of the same name, its position being 7 miles from Machynlleth on the road that leads to Mallwyd. Its position is compact and attractive on a flat, raised glade on the edge of the River Dyfi. Far away on one side can be seen Moel Eiddew, rising its crested peak to greet the firmament; and on the other side of the Dyfi, on the northern side, the hills of Llanwrin are seated to feast their eyes for evermore on the charming beauty of the fertile valley that touches their feet. Here stands the Parish church, on the edge of a hollow, past whose foot the Dyfi flows slowly along on its journey.

Not often can a church and graveyard be seen in such a pleasant position. The most common opinion is that it is dedicated to St. Tydecho, but Mr Nicholas Carlisle believes that it is dedicated to St Michael. The income is in the incumbency of the diocese of Llanelwy. The Calvinistic Methodists have a capacious house of worship here. There are two clean and tidy hotels here, where the stranger on his journey can have a place to rest in peace and comfort, and for a reasonable price. The post office is kept in the hotel of Mr Ryder, and the letters are dispatched daily at 4 in the afternoon. A four horse carriage, the *'Engineer'* runs through daily throughout the year. There are also several shops here, but the main industry is associated with treating wool, as well as agriculture. There are a National School and a British School here in a floral position.

Around the river and this place, a little further up, stands the farmhouse of Dolfonddu – the old farmhouse whose name was made so public in association with the Reverend William Jones, who, for many years, ministered with great commendation in the midst of the Calvinistic Methodists. Nearby is a small hill called Gallt-y-bont, which is extraordinary for the attention it attracts with changes in the weather. If it is in the middle of the cloudless sunshine of harvest, just a small glimpse of mist on *"Allt-y-bont"* makes everyone in the area instantly *"sure"* that *"rain is coming"*.

CILCWM See PENNANT

CLIPIAU

On the southern side of the River Angell stands this small village, 10½ miles from Machynlleth. Its houses are arranged higgledy-piggledy in the middle of fertile gardens, on the slope of a small, pretty hill that rises nearby. The main industry of the inhabitants derives from wool treatment.

COMMINS COCH

This village stands on the side of the River Twymin, 8 miles from Machynlleth, on the road to Y Drefnewydd [Newtown]. It is built at the foot of a small hill, in a curve not dissimilar to a horseshoe, such that it is necessary to go to the verge of each side before it is visible. It is apparent that it gets its name from the hill behind it, which is general waste land of the type that the Englishman calls "common"; and Commin is an adulteration of this English word. There is a hotel here, which is quite convenient as it is at the half-way point of the road from Llanbrynmair to Machynlleth. Nearby are an excellent watermill and a woollen factory. To the west of it is the chapel of Ty-cerig, a house of worship belonging to the Wesleyans. The village and its inhabitants commonly appear somewhat dingy, receiving their chief maintenance from the surrounding farms. Near to Commins Coch is the farmhouse of Castell Haiarn, the old dwelling of the bard and author of *The Welsh Grammar*, Sion Rhydderch.

CORRIS

If we start from Machynlleth over Bont-ar-Ddyfi, and take the road on our right hand side, which heads for Dolgellau, for around five miles, we come to the convenient Braichgoch Hotel, which stands by a crossroads, with one road leading to Dolgellau, and the other to the district of Corris. See **DULAS**. It is thought that the meaning of the word is *cor-ris – dwarf-stairs* or *'sheep stairs'*, which were beyond doubt numerous here before the howls of the wind frightened them off. While facing this remarkable district, very little attracts our attention except crested mountains, and the bare teeth of the rocks stretching out to meet us; but we see that the inhabitants are living peacefully, and enjoying the comfortable support of *"demolishing these uplands"*. The old houses in the neighbourhood are few and seldom – just one here and one there, like old relics from time gone by, when there was nothing to see except sheep making their homes on the slopes of the grey, etched hills, without the escarpment of one quarry to frighten them, and a multitude of soulless rural people living as they could in their houses below. But things have changed by now, and the severe and forlorn land of beauty has become a well of wealth.

The name Corris is commonly given to the area and the village together. The lower part is called Abercorris, because the river joins the Dulas nearby. It is made up of a host of houses, but they are not presented in the tidiest way. There are two large, attractive shops here, and numerous smaller ones. Nearby is a woollen factory. The Post Office here is kept in the house of Mr Robinson. A little below it is Rehoboth, a large and pretty chapel belonging to the Calvinistic Methodists, and a graveyard associated with it. There is also a hotel here.

If we travel along the main road for around a mile, we get a view of a small schoolhouse built at the expense of the inhabitants to hold a British School, and it is good to see it holding its own. A little further on is the machine for weighing loads of stone, etc. A little further again, and we are within sight of the farmhouse of Aberllefenny, which lurks modestly amongst the trees. It is a place of considerable dignified antiquity, and all its partitions - inside and out – are covered in many coats of arms of old Welsh Heroes, who kindled some patriotic warmth in the bosom of every lover of "Wales, the Welshman, and Welsh". Counsellor Flutton, the author of "History of Pembrokeshire", lived in it for a long time.

By now here we are by the marvellous crags of Aberllefenny, and we see hundreds of workers assiduously at it; some boring and splitting the rocks, others hauling the treasures out, and others preparing the goods to face different parts of the world; and truly they have succeeded significantly in making the place represent its name – Aber–llech–feini (river mouth of the slab stones).

There are many houses here, but they are quite scattered. The Calvinistic Methodists have a house of worship here. The stone from this quarry is so blue and lasting that it was chosen to build the *National Gallery* and numerous other public buildings. Around a mile from this place is the sturdy mansion called Hengae, which has been the residence of the Annwyl family for a long period.

On the road that leads to Dolgellau is a small village called Cae-y-wern, Upper and Lower, the former being up on the slope of a hill away from the road, and the other by the side of the road. Here J. W. Rowlands Esq., and his Company have many buildings, including machines to saw stone, etc. Also to be seen here is a *strange* thing – both in England and Wales – namely slates being polished in every kind of colour, until one can find one's own shadow in them – in *Chimney pieces, Round Tables, etc.* Higher up again can be found another part of the village called Glan-y-dery. Around a quarter of a mile further is a row of new houses built on

the side of the road, named after their owner, Mr Hills; Hillsburgh*.
Apart from these there are several other houses on the side, facing
the River Dulas, such as Ty'n-y-berth, Ty'n-y-ceunant, Pen-y-stair,
Hen-ffatri, etc.

In a place called Maesgorwydd in this district, on the flats on top of
the hill, it is said that the inhabitants of Dolgellau and Machynlleth
would meet each other to hold a fair. Nearby to this place are also
the remains of an old castle.

As suggested, it is the numerous and valuable quarries here that
raised the place to such popularity and attention. There are in
Corris five different quarries belonging to different owners; namely
Aberllefenny, Gaewern, Ty'nyberth, Ty'nceunant, and Braichgoch.
Belonging to them all are suitable houses and machines to make the
stones' appearance excellent before sending them from their hands.
So large is the demand for the slates and the expense of conveying
them to Derwenlas to reach the boats, and the current
inconvenience of taking domestic necessities to the inhabitants, that
it was decided to force a railway from here, through the Dulas
valley, past Machynlleth to Aberdyfi. Permission was given by
Parliament to do this, but unfortunately we have so far seen it
delayed.

Perhaps it would not be fair to continue without mentioning the
farmhouse of Braichgoch, the abode of Mr Evan Owen, son of Mr
Owen, formerly of Penygarreg, who was so famous for his
capabilities as a bone and joint doctor. The same craft was taken on
by his son, to the blessing of many near and far. The family, like
many other people, have been famous for ages for their abilities in

---

* This word derives from the Saxon word *beorgan*, indicating "to
patronize" "to defend" "to protect", such as St Petersburg, Edinburgh
[Edwin's burgh], etc.

this regard, which brings to mind the attention of one sensible man on another matter, *"Not from blood"* he said, *"but when it is seized in blood, it is not soon released".*

There is a high opinion about the position of the inhabitants nationally and religiously. Many a time a temperate shout and trumpet was given in the ears of the districts, and Oh! We cannot continue before *"pronouncing the truth as a blazing fire throughout our land,"* until the thousands that are dying of drunkenness hear the exclamation, and become alive.

Apart from the houses of worship I noted before, the Independents and Wesleyans have chapels on the side of the road that leads to Dolgellau. I cannot finish yet without quoting the lines of the bard Lewis Glyn Dyfi about *"Corris".*

> *Hen ardal serchiadol, ddymunol ei moes!*
> *Un fangre is awyr mwy difyr nid oes;*
> *Mae'n gweddu im' gynull it'bennill o parch*
> *Cyn myned i'r ceufedd i orwedd mewn arch.*
>
> *Ei serchus drigolion o galon, i gyd*
> *Am danynt pan gofiaf, ymrodda fy mryd*
> *I gyfrif adgofion tra llawnion sy'n llu*
> *Yn coffa llawenydd rhyw fwynddydd a fu.*
>
> *Rhwng bryniau mawr uchel yn dawel rhoed hi*
> *I ymladd â'r creigiau trwy rwystrau diri';*
> *A chael trwy eu chwalu, dan ganu yn gain,*
> *Gysurus fywioliaeth, wir helaeth o'r rhai'n.*

Mor hynod wrth basio yw gwrando ar gri
Y cedyrn glogwyni tra'n hollti yn llu!
Er iddynt ymdrechu, gan dyrddu yn dost,
Dan ddwylaw'r preswylwyr y baeddir eu bost!

Llechfeini dihafal yr ardal a ro'nt
I'w goror fri dinag lle bynag y b'ont;
Gan lawer pell bentref, a thref yn ei thro,
Canmolir ffrwyth creigiau llwyd fryniau'r hen fro.

Trwy'r ddwyfol Efengyl ddi-gynil ei gwaith,
Holl Gorris ddaw trwyddi i ddysgu'r dda iaith;
Bydd tônau ei Dirwest yn goncwest i gyd,
A'i noddfa fydd Prynwyr a Barnwyr y byd.

Old amiable district, so pleasant her wont!
There is no pleasanter a place 'neath the sun;
So fitting for me to sing you a verse
Before I lay down in my coffin of rest.

When I remember the ones who I once
Knew well, those hearty inhabitants, I count
The memories of yore, before I hark back
To the laughter and smiles of days gone by.

Between the lofty hills she was laid
To grapple with boulders and rocks everywhere;
And to have from the stones, whilst singing so fine,
Once shattered, a living so fair.

So wondrous, when passing, to listen to cries
Of cliffs and crags falling down from above!

Although they may strive and struggle the more,
In the hands of these dwellers they fall from the skies!

The stones of the valley give virtuous renown
To her unrivalled quarry wherever they be;
The crop from the hills and the grey hordes above
Are praised and exalted in all manner of towns.

Through the work of the Gospel in every one
All Corris will prosper to learn the good tongue;
Her Temperate tones will conquer all else,
The Redeemer and Saviour of all be her light.[2]

CADER IDRIS

This mountain is the second highest in Wales: it is 2914 feet above the surface of the sea. It rises from the seaside, near the north side of the River Dysynwy, around a mile from Tywyn, and runs in northern and north-easterly directions, in a line of high mountains, including the Aran and Arenig. It is extremely steep and rocky on every side, but the southerly part that faces Tal-y-llyn is the most dangerous because it is almost perfectly sheer.

It is likely that it got its name from the Giant Idris, who the triads say was one of the *"three white sorcerers of the island of Britain"*. We are told that the giant studied the heavenly bodies from this mountain, for which reason it is given its name – Cader Idris (Idris' Seat).

We are told that at its highest point there is a hollow cavern in the rock, not dissimilar to a chair, whoever spends a night on which will by morning either be dead, insane, or inspired!

It is normally from Dolgellau that the journey to its peak is taken;

and as I have not so far had the privilege of climbing it, you will forgive me for setting in front of the reader the story of the ascent of a familiar traveller.

Mr Pugh, author of the *"Cambria Depicta"* says:

> *"It was on a fair morning when I ascended Cadair Idris myself. I took the lower road to Tywyn for three miles, then turned towards the mountain, through an enclosed wood, gaining the sunlit land; I made my way over a place called the 'cyfrwy' ('saddle') until I came to a large plain, and after a slow climb for around a mile, I found myself on top of the highest cliff. I cannot be more favourable about the clearness, excellence, and cloudlessness I enjoyed. The views that can be had from it of all the surroundings are of unperceivable beauty. To the north can be seen Snowdon, on the uncultivated breast of which often can be seen the tired clouds resting, standing above their friends while showing their broad sides, which appear as if they are commanding respect from all.*
> *To the east can be seen the fertile plains of Shropshire, and the interlaying mountains of the Trefaldwyn county (Montgomeryshire). To the south we find Pumlummon and the surrounding mountains"*

Mr Warner said:

> *"Independently of these distant objects, the neighbouring views are very striking. An uncomfortable number of mountains of different form, looks, and height, rising in all directions around us, which, along with the various harbours, lakes and rivers, towns, villages, and mansions*

scattered around the countryside in front of us, join in unison to form an unperceivable view of majesty".

"After satisfying our curiosity" said Mr Atkin,

"and having been totally chilled by the air of these high parts, we start to descend along the side opposite the one ascended. The first resting place takes us to the side of a beautiful lake, the cold water of which discharges its adequacy down in a waterfall along the side of the mountain. By following the waterfall we came to the midst of steep rocks, which face Talyllyn, and after a long and intricate journey we at last reached the verges of Talyllyn, where we went to the Dolgellau Road"

CRAIG-Y-DERYN

Named such after the large variety of cormorants, hawks and other birds of prey we observe on it*. The rock shoots up around 200 feet, away from the slope, which is covered in giant rocks; its height from the bottom is 700 feet. It is situated around 4 miles from Tywyn, and it is worth travelling a few miles in order to climb it, and take note of the variety of the winged host. The traveller Pennant ate his lunch under the high rock. I am certain that the reader will forgive me for quoting some of the Reverent Evan Evans' *(Ieuan Brydydd Hir)* verses for this excellent rock; they are as follows:-

---

* Craig-y-Deryn = Bird-Rock (NIDF)

Llyn-y-Cau, Cader Idris, by Richard Wilson[*]

Bryn yr Aderyn ar diroedd – uchel –
 Ichaf man dan nefoedd;
 Caer[†] gynt yn y creigiau oedd
 I filwyr mewn rhyfeloedd

Mae'r fran a'r aran ar oror – y graig
 Yn groew'n eu tymhor;
 Unan' yn gân un gor –
 Peraidd yw llais pob paror.

---

[*] See Penegoes (NIDF)
[†] Teberri Castle

Miwsig sy ddiddig i ddyn – naturiol
Yw cantorion telyn;
Melusach, rhwyddach er hyn
Yw 'daraeth Craig aderyn.

Bryn yr Aderyn (Bird's Hill) on high land –
The most wholesome place on earth;
Once a castle in the rocks
For soldiers of wars.

The crow and the crane on the rock's precipice
Are distinct in their season;
They sing together in one choir –
Sweet is the voice of each pair.

Music is pleasing for a man – natural also
Are the players of harps;
But sweeter and swifter
Is the birds' song on Craig Aderyn (Bird Rock).[2]

CWMLLINAU

A small village on the road from Cemmaes to Mallwyd, 9 miles from Machynlleth. The name is derived from the fact that it is a long village in a narrow valley, with the small River Llinau running through it. This arises in the nearby mountains, and with floods of rain it often swells so unexpectedly that its strong, frantic torrent, with stupendous noise, rolls the large stones of its bed like shells before it.

The village is positioned on the edge of this rivulet, which discharges into the Dyfi nearby. The main labour of the inhabitants is spinning and weaving wool. There are two chapels; one Wesleyan and the other Independent. Nearby this place, in a flat glade on the edge of the Dyfi, stands the pretty mansion of Dol-y-corslwyn, the present resident of which is Joseph Owen Jones Esq., the son of D Jones Esq., Parkllwydiarth. A little away from this village resides the bard Lewis Meredith, or Lewis Glyn Dyfi, author of *"The Flowers of Dyfi Vale"*.

CWMGLANMYNACH

This is the name of a long, deep valley that rises between the mountains away from Aberangell village. It comprises a large multitude of farms; and next to the furthest of these, namely Blaen-y-cwm, there grow a host of yew trees, quite ancient in their appearance, nearby which, as well as other signs, and the name of the valley, it is reckoned there was formerly an old monastery. Also, the name of a farm nearby the aforementioned one confirms this, namely Cae'r-batty – field of the abbot-house, or monastery. Also, on the slope of a small hill nearby, pieces of joints and men's skulls have been dug from the ground.

CYFEILIOG

The manor and hundred in the westerly part of Trefaldwyn county (Montgomeryshire). It includes the following six parishes:- Machynlleth, Cemmaes, Llanwrin, Penegoes, Darowen, and Llanbrynmair. It was previously included in the Principality of Powys, and it was assaulted to notable severity at the time of the Prince Owain Cyfeiliawg, who made his court here (SEE

TAFOLWERN). Mention is made of the thirteen towns of Cyfeiliog[*], but I am not in possession of any history about them at present, and perhaps they refer to other parts of the lands of Gruffydd ab Gwenwynwyn as well as Cyfeiliog. The current Lord of the Manor is Sir W. W. Wynne. The main town of the hundred is Machynlleth, and it is there that legal cases related to the area are heard.

DAROWAIN

A parish in the hundred of Cyfeiliog, 6 miles from Machynlleth. The meaning of the name is Derw Owain (Owain's Oak); but we have no information about that oak or its owner. It includes the tithe-townships of Carnseddfan and Noddfa.

There is a particular peculiarity associated with the latter tithe-township. Due to its name[†], it is thought that the church of the parish and the main land around it, which is marked out by three stones, is a place of safety for offenders of the national laws, or that they are something similar to the Sanctuary Lands formerly of Israel. These stones stand around a mile from the church; one of them is called "Careg Noddfa" ("Sanctuary Stone"), to the east; another, with a great deal of it above ground, to the south, and another much smaller, to the northeast.

The church stands in a small village, on the high mountainous land, called Llan Darowen. It is built in the early Saxon fashion, and it is dedicated to St Tudyr, who lived here[‡]. This Tudyr was the son of Arwystl loff ap Seithinin Frenin, by Dwywannedd, the daughter of Amlawd Wledig, who flourished in the 7th Century. The livelihood is in the diocese of Llanelwy. It was built in 1545 by the Bishop Robert

---

* Myfyriau Archaiology, cyf ii., page 464
† Noddfa = sanctuary/refuge (NIDF)
‡ Pedigree of the Saints of the Island of Britain

Warton under the instruction of Richard ab Gruffydd. It has been in the possession of Dr Davies, Mallwyd, Dr Randolph, and Dr Luxmore. For the endowments of the Parish see CEMMAES. The circulating Welsh Schools were established here in 1831. These schools were established by the Reverend Griffith Jones, Llanddowror, at the beginning of the 18th Century, and are supported by a host of Wales' gentry in this excellent task. They are moved from place to place every two years.

Standing stone south of Darowen, with Creigiau Rhosygarreg in the background

The Calvinistic Methodists have a house of worship in the village, and the Independents have one close by. There is also a National School and a beautiful handsome new schoolhouse.

There is a convenient Hotel to deal with matters of the parish and comfort those who happen to be on a journey this way. The road that leads to the village is steep, rugged, and unpleasant, and the parish-dwellers are much to be blamed for not making an effort to better it. Within half a mile of the village, to its west, on a hill near the farmhouse of Frongoch, there are the remains of an old camp; and on top of another hill called Bwlch-gelli-las there is a cairn, nearby which, on the sloping pasture of Berllan-deg, old military arms of Welsh manufacture were found some years ago.

The population of the parish in 1851 was 1119.

DERWENLAS

A small village two miles to the southwest of Machynlleth, built on the side of the road that leads from Machynlleth to Aberystwyth, and facing the River Dyfi, which is navigable to here by vessels carrying around 70 tonnes.

Its name derives from a large oak, which grew opposite, but was thrown down by the river, and its roots can still be seen in the water. It is of great convenience to the tradesmen of Machynlleth and the surrounding land, because it receives goods and conveys minerals and other things to reach ships in Aberdyfi. It is also convenient for building ships. In the village there are houses of worship owned by the Calvinistic Methodists, Independents and Wesleyans.

A tidy hotel is kept here by Mr Rees Williams. There are also several lime kilns. Many of the inhabitants make a living from fishing in the Dyfi during the summer months.

DOLGADFAN

A tithe-townshp in the parish of Llanbrynmair. There is also a small village of the same name, built in a wooded valley with the River Twymyn running through it. It is thought that the name derives not from Saint Cadfan, but from a battle fought in a meadow nearby*. The bard Gwilym Cyfeiliog resided here. Numerous shops can be found here, and woollen works. There are houses of worship owned by the Calvinistic Methodists and the Independents.

Derwenlas in the early 19th Century

---

* Cadfan = Name of a Welsh Saint. Gad-fan = place of battle (NIDF)

DOLGUOG

This is a farmhouse 1½ miles from Machynlleth on the edge of the confluence of the Rivers Dulas and Dyfi. The name is immortalised because one of the *"Three wise council knights of Arthur's Court"*, the famous bard Llywarch Hen, resided there. Llywarch flourished at around the end of the sixth and beginning of the seventh centuries. Having endeavoured gallantly on behalf of Urien Rheged, the Prince of Cumberland, in the north of England, he saw many of his men fall to the sword, and many of them fled with him to Cynddylan, son of Cyndrwyn, of the tribe of Ffrochwel Ysgythrog, the Prince of Powys. After Cynddylan had warred and fallen in his effort against the Saxons, the bard mournfully proclaimed:

Ystafell Cynddylan ys tywyll heno
Heb dân heb deulu –
Hidl mau yd gynu !

Ystafell Cynddylan a'm gwân ei gweled
Heb doed, heb dân –
Marw fy nglyw, byw my hunan !

Ystafell Cynddylan ys tywyll heno,
Gwedi colli ei hynaf –
Y mawr drugarawg Dduw pa wnaf !

The hall of Cynddylan is dark tonight,
No fire, no household.
Free flow my tears where night falls.

The hall of Cynddylan, the sight stabs me,
No rooftop, no fire.
Dead my lord, myself alive.

The hall of Cynddylan is tame tonight,
Having lost its ruler.
God of mercy, what shall I do? [4]

After that he composed poetry for Cuog ab Cyndrwyn, Cynddylan's brother, who possessed an heirdom on the banks of the Dulas, which was called Cuog at that time. Here the old man used to stroll the lengths of the green meadows in the gentle breeze, and it is without doubt that he did not infrequently sit on some cliff to touch on the strings of the enchanting harp, and relieve his sorrows through the aid of his powerful muse. His poems to the *"Cuckoo in Abercuawg"* should be in the memory of every one of the inhabitants of our land, in respectful remembrance of him; they are as follows;

Cog lafar a gan min dydd,
Cyfreu eichiawg yn nolydd Cuawg –
Gwell corawg na chybydd.

Yn y fan uwch llon dar
Ydd endewais i lais adar:
Cog fan cof gan bawb a gar.

A loud cuckoo sings at dawn,
A clear song in the dales of Cuawg,
Better a spendthrift than miser.

On the height above the mighty oak
I listened to birds' voices.
Cuckoo loud; what they love, all remember.[3]

Mr Jones states in his *"Welsh Bards"* that Llywarch Hen died here at 150 years old, but Dr John Davies attests that it was in Llanfawr, near Bala, that this took place, and he states that he saw an engraving on the wall of that church, under which it states that Llywarch Hen's body was laid to rest.

DULAS (NORTH)

This crystal-clear river forms from numerous small streams that originate in the rocks of Corris, and discharges into the Dyfi near Machynlleth. Because few minerals are extracted in its surroundings it contains a plenitude of handsome and delicious fish, and there is freedom for everyone to fish in it. I cannot give a better description of the valley and the main road that goes through it than the following words:

> *"Our road was at first through a quite deep valley, along the bottom of which, under our right hand side, roared the sparkling river, travelling in the opposite direction to us. Here we had exceptionally beautiful views with the steep slopes of the valley each side of us sometimes bare and harsh, other times coarse and rocky, but mostly clad by small oaks. I often was afraid of finding our way blocked between the hills. The occasional chunk of hill would have seated itself down as a bundle in a narrow place, threatening us; 'to here you will go and no further'. But having gone up to it and pressed a bit on its knee, it would quietly release us to go past. We before long reached a slate works*".*

In this valley, a little below Abercorris, stands the small pretty mansion of Fronfelen, the former residence of D. P. Evans Esq., a

---

* Traethodydd, cyf. viii. Page 426

reputable doctor, who was for many years of great benefit to the area because of his medical abilities. A little lower down is the beautiful mansion of Llwyngwern, the dwelling of F. J. Ford Esq., who is notable as an agriculturalist, and a hearty supporter of horticulture, herbiculure, and general culture, and he keeps a multitude of the poor in work. Near this place a free day-school is held for poor children. Also along the banks of the river are several woollen factories and mills. Lately, an Act of Parliament was passed to create a railway through this beautiful valley to Aberdyfi, and I trust that this will be completed with haste.

DULAS (SOUTH)

A little to the east, beyond the River Dyfi, a stream of the same name discharges into the Dyfi. This originates from the flows of Glaslyn lake and flows down through quite romantic valleys, receiving assistance from a host of small streams, such as the Carog, Talbontdrain, Crewi, etc., until it reaches the Dyfi near Machynlleth. On its banks are built the villages of Forge and Pontfelingerig, and there are no fewer than thirteen factories, between mills, fulling mills, and woollen factories, turned by it on its journey.

Its fish are not numerous in its upper parts, but they are handsome trout, especially as the Dyfi is approached.

DYFI

The word derives from *dof-wy*, or docile flow, quiet, smooth-running; and the river is truly like this. This splendid river flows from a black, dark and deep lake at the foot of Aran Fawddwy and its surrounding area to within about a mile. For the first mile of its journey it is called the *Llaethnant (milk-stream)*, and the valley through which it flows is called *Cwm-llaeth (milk-valley)*, from the tradition that Saint Tydecho, who lived here, and was remarkable for his magical powers, turned it into milk to satisfy the need of the poor; and the following lines have immortalised the tradition:

> *Tydecho dad di duchan*
> *A'i gwnaeth yn llaeth hyd y llan.*

> *Tydecho, untiring father,*
> *Turned her to milk as far as the village.*[2]

The first part of the journey of this beautiful river is wild and roaring, making its way through the clefts and mounds that stand in its way. By Bont Mallwyd its appearance is marvellous, dashing dreadfully on the rocks that lie in the middle of its bed, roaring dangerously as it goes past, as if in a rush to escape its chains. Yea, as the author of *"Blodau Glyn Dyfi"* sang:

> *Er fod clogwyni gwyllt yr Aran serth*
> *Ar ddechreu'th daith, mewn blin sarugrwydd certh,*
> *Yn hongian uwch dy ben, a chreigiau fyrdd*
> *Yn ceisio'th attal i dy ddyffryn gwyrdd –*
> *Buddugol wyt ar eu holl rwystrau hwy,*
> *Ac wedi cyraedd hon nid ofni mwy;*
> *Pleserus bellall fydd dy araf daith*
> *Rhwng dolydd hyfryd, a gweirgloddiau maith,*
> *Nes cyraedd mynwes ddofn yr eigion llaith.*

> *Although the wild cliffs of the steep Aran*
> *Stand at your journey's beginning, bold and surly,*

So menacing above, and although the rocks
May stand between you and your valley green, –
You will surpass their many stumbling blocks,
And once you reach this one, fear no more;
Pleasant evermore will be your winding way
Between the meadows and the blooming fields,
Until you reach the great bosom of the sea.[2]

Its water is clear like crystal, its bed untarnished gravel, and its banks pleasant and pleasing, and it greatly surpasses most of the rivers of Wales. Because of the abundance of its fish – salmon, gwyniaid[*], trout etc., a large multitude of gentlemen who visit it daily testify highly of it.

There is not the freedom for everyone to fish in it, but those who pay the following for tickets can do so, but only with a fly:

	£	s	d
For the season	2	2	0
For a month	1	0	0
For a week	0	7	6
For a day	0	2	0

It is open to fishing on the 1st of April, and closes on the 14th of December. Four water bailiffs are kept on it consistently, and it has been under strict management for the past 10 years.

The tickets, as well as all additional information, can be obtained from Mr C. J. Lloyd, Machynlleth.

Regarding the vale through which the river slowly meanders, it

---

[*] By *gwyniaid* the author is likely to be referring to sea trout; however, the name *gwyniad* is nowadays used to refer specifically to a species of whitefish that exists only in Llyn Tegid (Bala Lake) (NIDF)

compares in natural beauty with any in Wales – and England as well, apparently. The vale of Clwyd is far more expansive, but also wetter on its surface, and more lifeless in its appearance. The vales of Meifod and Llangollen can boast of their beauty, yet they are only small glades when they compete with the vale of Dyfi, which boasts twenty five miles in length, from Llanymawddwy to Aberdyfi, and almost three miles in breadth, from Pont Llyfnant to Gogarth. But it is not only of the incomparable breadth and beauty of its river that it can boast; it is surrounded on all sides by green hills, its slopes falling gradually towards it, like fertile cultivated agricultural gardens, about which it is varied by patches of young trees, which are a considerable addition to the beauty of the views. These are embraced in the bosom of the beautiful vale below, and all the clean villages, cultivated farms, and the splendid residencies and their beauty. And, regarding the quality of its inhabitants, I cannot do better than use the words of one bard:

O lawer tro dy don fu'n dyst, er pan
Fu awen Llywarch Hen yn canu ar dy lan;
Ar foesau'th finion cyfnewyd mawr
Gymerodd le o hyny hyd yn awr;
Yn lle yr hardd, ond gwledig, symledd pur,
I blith pob gradd daeth oeraidd falchder sur;
Yn awr gan fawr a bach, mewn gwisg a moes,
Y nod o hyd yw coeglyd ddull yr oes.
Ond gwelaist hefyd hen arferion fil
O flaen eu gwell yn gorfod myn'd ar gil:
Godyrddain nefol ffrydiau gras ein Duw
Sy'n awr er's blwyddau maith yn adsain yn dy glyw

Many a change did your waters witness,
Since Llywarch Hen once sang upon your banks;

To your borders's morals a great change has come
To pass between the days of yore and now;
Instead of the sightly, if rural, simple land,
And into every place, came pride so cold and sour;
And now do every one in all their manners
Aspire to the vain routine and customs of the age.
But you also saw the practices of yore
Retreating to make way for others yet:
The roaring of God's heavenly founts of grace
Are now, since many years, resounding all around.[2]

A host of heroes who made themselves notable in the inventory of history were raised in the valley, such as Llywarch Hen, Dafydd Llwyd ab Llewelyn ab Gruffydd, Mathafarn; Ieuan Dyfi, Aberdyfi; Robyn Dyfi, Glandyfi; William Dyfi; Dr John Davies, Mallwyd; Mr Davies, tutor of the Grammatical School, Macclesfield; etc., and I am confident that not a few will rise in it again to immortalise themselves.

DYLIFAU[*]

A mountainous area between Machynlleth and Llanidloes, 10 miles from the former. The road that leads to it is one of the most rugged and wild on the British island. Perhaps the name arises from the flows of the frantic floods of the rivulets from here down the valleys at rainy and tempestuous times[†]. The natural position of the area holds nothing tempting to attract men to live in it, as it mostly consists only of wet and bare peat-land. And if it were not for the rich seams of minerals found lying in the bowels of its ground, it is

---

[*] Now known as Dylife (NIDF)
[†] Dylifau = flows or floods (NIDF)

probable enough that there would not be any significant number of inhabitants, except for shepherds and the like. But because of that already alluded to, numerous new houses have been built, here and around the area, in the midst of the old ones, such that it is presently a flourishing neighbourhood, and the number of inhabitants is numerous and plentiful.

The place is savage and cold in the winter, but wholesome and pleasant in the summer. The main lead works are Llechwedd-du, Esgairgaled, Dyfngwm, and Bryn-y-fedwen. By Esgairgaled is the largest waterwheel in the known world – 60 feet in diameter – and it pays well for the trouble of going to see it.

Because the churches of the closest parishes are a long way from this place, it was decided that a new church should be built here, in a small village called Rhydwen – which is now finished. The Baptists and Calvinistic Methodists have houses of worship in the area. On the side of the main road nearby is the convenient hotel of Camder-y-ffordd.

Around a mile and a half from Dylifau, in a small valley called Berkin, near the farmhouse of Llwyn-y-gog, stands an old castle, and I have heard some of the inhabitants call it Castell Elin. I do not at present have any information about this Elin. It is now in ruins, and a lake covers where it stood. About the old castle there are six or eight large mounds, or as they are commonly called "Tomenau Gleision" (Green Mounds), and it is commonly judged that they were defensive towers. Away from the old castle a stone road went over Pumlimmon to Aberystwyth, and many parts of this are to be seen to this day.

Dylife as it was in the latter part of the 19ᵗʰ Century

EGLWYSFACH – or SCUBOR-Y-COED

A part of the land in the parish of Llanfihangel-geneu'r-glyn, Ceredigion (Cardiganshire), standing on the eastern side of the small River Einion, close to its junction with the Dyfi. The country is commonly wooded, and excellent views can be had from some parts of it. Going towards Eglwysfach, around 5 miles to the west of Machynlleth, this side of the bridge over the small rivulet that runs from the nearby mountains, we turn our gaze upwards on our left-hand side; here is the old mansion of Dyfi Bank, the current resident of which is D. Wolsey Esq., who, along with his wife, is a member of the Wesleyans, and has for many years offered no small aid to the cause in the area.

Up here, out of sight, is Melin Dyfi Bank, in which, some 70 years ago, one Charmer, a gentleman from Llynlleifiaid (Liverpool), took on dusty and smoky work, while living in Dyfi Bank. By the bridge there is a bunch of houses on the side of the road. Going on again, around a quarter of a mile, we find the farmhouse of Dolen-Eglwys on our right-hand side. On again is the village, about which there is not much of anything to say, except that there are a few somewhat poorly looking houses on both sides of the road. There is a shop here in which is kept the Post Office. At the foot of the hill, away from the village, stands the chapel of the Wesleyans. At the foot of the hill, further on, is the church of the parish, or Llanfihangel Capel Edwin, which is a beautiful new church dedicated to Saint Michael. The old church, which was notably small, and after which the village was named*, was built early in the seventeenth century. A famous bard called Wmffre Owen was for a long period a minister in this church.

The famous Thomas Jones, Creaton, one of the founders of the Biblical Society, was also inaugurated here in September 1744. Like most godly priests who worked at that time, he received only poor recognition for his hard labour, which is a good reason why he moved from his country of birth. He said to a friend in his old age that *"I was inaugurated as a curate in Wales for twenty pounds a year"*. It was asked of him whether that was his wage. *"Yes, and I lived well on it; I gave six pounds for my board and lodgings, six pounds for clothes, three pounds for grazing for my horse on the mountains, and a pound in charities"*. The narrator cannot remember what was done with the remaining four pounds[†].

We go over a bridge again, and we are in *Furnace*, above which a rivulet flows frantically over a high rock. There are only a small

---

* Eglwys Fach = Small Church (NIDF)
[†] Llyfr y Jubili, by the Reverend T Phillips, page 112

number of somewhat poorly looking houses here, each side of the road. The ruined wall of the old furnace, from which the village gets its name, stands near the aforementioned bridge. They used to smelt iron in this place, and it was worked until some 60 years ago by one Mr Candell. It was not possible to get coal here, for which reason charcoal was transported from Ganllwyd, the other side of Dolgellau.

FFORGE – See PONTFAEN

FFRWD FAWR – See PENNANT

GARREG

A small mooring on the Dyfi, around 5 miles to the southwest of Machynlleth. The sea here is navigable by vessels of 300 tonnes. The village receives its name from a sizable rock in the middle of the river, by the village, known by the name Careg-y-lliw, Careg-estyn-llaeth, and Careg-ystym-lladd. The old ferryman, John Felix, says that the meaning of the name careg estyn llaeth* is as follows; many years ago the river was very narrow in the place where the stone is, and much commerce occurred at that time between the counties of Meirionnydd (Merioneth) and Ceredigion (Cardiganshire), and the inhabitants of the former county would, because the river was so narrow, lower milk from the rock to those in the latter county.

In relation to the other name, careg ystym lladd, it is said that on this rock was killed a lion that had been reared in the Llyfnant valley, the name of which, incidentally, signifies the valley of the *Llew-nant (Lion-stream).*

The minerals excavated in the Royal works in Ceredigion

---

* Careg estyn llaeth = milk passing stone (NIDF)

(Cardiganshire) were smelted in foundries at this place. The village stands as two rows of houses each side of the main road, in the shadow of a wooded hill, on the slopes of which can be seen, on the lower side of the village, beautiful evergreen plants. Up on the hill, like a monarch on its elevated throne, stands Dyfi Castle, the residence of George Jeffreys Esq. On the side of the road between this village and Eglwysfach stands the small pleasant mansion of Edward Jeffreys Esq., in front of which can be seen two tall Cypresses, not so much commonly seen, raising their pointed heads towards heaven.

GLASBWLL

Around 2 miles from Machynlleth, amidst the mountains, stands this unnoticed small village.

As we approach it we go past the excellent new mansion of Garthgwynion, the residence of Mr M E Lewis, which is a beautiful building in the middle of broad flat land; and the owner went to considerable expense to repair and cultivate this place. A little further on, on our left hand side, away from the road, is the pretty Wesleyan house of worship, and near this, on the side of the road, are a few labourers' cottages. A little further, and we are by the mansion of Cae'rsaer, which is totally enclosed by trees, and is the residence of Thomas Lewis Esq.; a generous and obliging gentleman, universally highly respected by the inhabitants of the area. Near this place is a house of worship owned by the Independents. There are many houses here apart from this, as well as a woollen factory.

The main employment of the inhabitants derives from working on the surrounding farms. The River Llyfnant runs through the area, irrigating it well, driven by another stream from Cefncoch.

*Cwm Rhaeadr (valley of the waterfall), at
the head of the Llyfnant valley*

GLASLYN

A black, round lake, around a mile in circumference, closer to
Machynlleth than Bugeilyn by a mile. Every fish perishes as soon as
it is put into this lake because of some poison that apparently
emanates from the mineral substances that are throughout its
sediment. This is the source of the River Dulas.

GWIDOL

A river that rises at the foot of Bwlch-clin-mynydd, and, having flowed several miles, through mostly deep valleys, discharges into the Dyfi by the farmhouse of Abergwydol.

The following can be found in the Triads: *"The three fiendish bulls of the island of Britain, the fiend Gwidawl, and the fiend Llyr Merini, and the fiend Gwrthmwl Wledig"*, and it appears that it is from the former, the name of which signifies *"The fiend of the frantic stream"*, from Gwy: *flow*, and dawl: *hurl, spark, etc.,* that this river got its name. On its banks are seated the villages of Talywern, Dol-y-bont, and Abercegir. Near its conjunction with the River Dyfi stands the large and beautiful farmhouse of Abergwidol, which is unusually convenient for accommodating gentlemen who wish to enjoy the diversion of fishing in these fish-filled rivers.

IS-Y-GARREG

A tithe-township in the parish of Machynlleth, around two miles to the southwest of Machynlleth town. From some parts of it a pleasant view can be seen of the River Dyfi, meandering through the fruitful vale, from Cemmaes to the sea-inlets of Ceredigion (Cardiganshire). Most of it is mountainous, wild, and uncultivated, especially those domains that tend towards Ceredigion (Cardiganshire). A portion of the township has the right to vote in association with the borough of Machynlleth. Many excellent mine-workings can be found in it. The population in 1851 was 415.

LERI

A river that rises in the mountains of the parish of Llanfihangel-geneu'r-glyn, and meets the Ceulan near Tal-y-bont.

LLANBRYNMAIR

A broad parish in the hundred of Cyfeiliog, 11 miles long and 7 miles wide, consisting of the tithe-townships of Dolgadfan, Pennant, Tir-y-myneich, Tafolwern, and Rhiw-saeson.

Despite being mostly steep and mountainous, delightful flats and fair valleys can be found there, and it can compete with any area in Wales for a great sight of farmhouses and agriculture. The most

Wynnstay Arms, now known as Llanbrynmair,
viewed from Newydd Fynyddog

extreme regions such as have been recognised can be found in this neighbourhood; here can be seen high, crested mountains, rising proudly towards heaven, and the small, fertile hills, being crowned with beautiful lines of green wooded slopes. In it can be found the closed wooded valley, and the flat, irrigated vale. It is smattered with small enclosed glades, and spacious, open flats. Dispersed through it are cleanly farmhouses, encompassed by fertile and cultivated land, and lively and valuable workplaces. This demonstrates, to a great degree, the consistency of the mind of the inhabitants, who always prove themselves to be opposers of aggression and tyranny, and warm partisans of National and religious freedom, and they show a strong desire to drive darkness and ignorance from the land, and to cultivate light and virtue.

The church of the parish stands on top of a small round hill, from which it is likely the name Llan-bryn-mair is derived*, the church being dedicated to Mary. It is said that its history can be traced back as far as the eleventh century, and in it are several examples of old oak carvings, and in the graveyard are some very old yew trees.

At some time around the middle of the sixteenth century, an old bard by the name of Wmffre Dafydd ab Ifan was a bell ringer in this church, and William Phylip, another bard from Ardudwy in Meirionnydd (Merioneth), decided to come here to look for his friend. When he came near to the village he asked a boy whether he would show him Wmffre Dafydd ab Ifan's house. He answered that he would, then led him to the graveyard, and after coming to a new grave said to him *"this is Wmffre Dafydd ab Ifan's house!"* The circumstances and words had such a profound effect on the mind of the bard that, having turned away on his journey sad and disappointed, he composed that part of his work called *"cywydd* of the Grave".

---

* Llan bryn Mair = Church of Mary's hill

In the year 1782 Morgan Llwyd Esq. endowed the annual production of a smallholding in the parish of Trefeglwys to the care of the Vicar and the guardian of this parish, for the purpose of being shared amongst goodly purposes, and the trustees have committed one part of it towards supporting a daily school, and the other part to be distributed between the poor.

The Independents and Calvinistic Methodists have several chapels throughout the parish, but the biggest as a building, and the oldest in terms of its establishment, and the most recognised everywhere, is the "Hen Gapel" ("Old Chapel"), owned by the Independents, associated with which is a graveyard. A daily school is also kept here. The chapel stands on a wooded slope, a little way from the main road that leads to Y Drefnewydd (Newtown).

Many famous and resourceful old ministers were ministers here, such as Lewis Rees, Richard Tibbot, and John Roberts; and the current minister, the son of the venerable John Roberts, namely the learned, talented, and extremely well known Samuel Roberts AC, is no less famous or resourceful. A few years ago the members of the chapel felt it their duty to do something to show their respect for the memory of the old commendable fathers who shepherded them. Money was collected and a marble memorial was erected which was set behind the pulpit, and inscribed on it is the reason for its erection, and verses by Gwilym Hiraethog, one of which is as follows:

> Rees hyglod, Tibbot, dad hybarch, - a Roberts,
> Dri arabawl Batriarch,
> Tri a gofir trwy gyfarch
> Hyd oes byd, gyda dwys barch.

> Renowned Rees, Tibbot, venerable father, – and Roberts,
> Three joyous Patriarchs,

Three who are remembered by addressing them
With deep respect all through the age of the world.[2]

It would not be fair to pass on without alluding to the fact that the son of the aforesaid Lewis Rees was Dr Abraham Rees, who is so highly famed in the area of English literature. He was born here in the year 1742, and he intended, when young, to move towards the work of the ministry. He was under the tutorship of Dr Jenkin Jenkins, in the educational institute of Caerfyrddin (Carmarthen), and from there went to Hoxton, near London. His progress was so fast in terms of teaching that he was not yet twenty years old when he was chosen as a mathematics teacher in that school, a position he held for 22 years.

After that, he ministered with the Presbyterians. But it is his characteristic literature rather than his ministerial character that has brought him to attention. The main literary pursuit that he completed was composing and editing a cyclopaedia, which came about as follows: in the year 1776 the owners of *Chambers Cyclopaedia* wished to publish an extended edition of the same, and it was agreed with Dr Rees that he would edit the venture, which was honourably completed in nine years, and brought out in four large complete volumes.

He was heaped with such praise that the owners were inspired to further extend the work again, and the Doctor agreed to edit it. He started on a new Encyclopaedia, on another broader quarto form, and this totalled forty five volumes – to that magnitude! It was called from then on *Rees's Encyclopaedia,* and doubtless it will last as a special memento of his learnedness and talents throughout all the ages.

He was the author of numerous profound books and essays. He received the title of Doctor of Theology from Edinburgh University, and the specific encouragement of Dr W. Robertson, the historian.

He was also a member of numerous praiseworthy and Royal Associations. He died on June the 9th, 1825, having reached the age of 82 years.

By *Wynnstay Arms,* a small village* on the side of the road that leads to Y Drefnewydd (Newtown), popular fairs are held on the following days each year: the Monday before the last Tuesday in March, the Tuesday before the third Thursday in April, May the 31st, September the 30th, and November the 11th.

There is a cleanly and convenient Hotel here, in which the post-house is kept. Fairs are held by the church on the following days: The Friday before the first fair in Welshpool in March, May the 31st, September the 16th, and November the 25th. This small village stands in a pretty location, near the church of the parish, and there is a comfortable hotel in it.

LLANCYNFELYN

A parish in the upper part of the hundred of Geneu'rglyn, Ceredigion (Cardiganshire), around 11 miles from Machynlleth. It runs alongside the River Dyfi, which is navigable in this place, and so convenient to ship out considerable mineral wealth, and other things that are sent away from here in great plenitude.

The church, which is dedicated to Saint Cynfelyn, was built in the early 6th century, but was recently rebuilt from new. The benefice is a perpetual curacy in the Archdeaconry of Ceredigion (Cardiganshire), in the diocese of Saint David's, and under the patronage of the Chichester family, in Devonshire. The Calvinistic Methodists and Independents have houses of worship in the parish.

---

* This village is now known as *Llanbrynmair,* while the original village of Llanbrynmair is known as *Llan*

As indicated, there are a multitude of fruitful mineral workings in this parish, some, apparently, having been open since very early times. When Sir Hugh Middleton took on Esgair-hir mineral workings, we are told by Mr Pugh, of Ty Gwyn, near Machynlleth, the following history, which may be of some interest to readers:

In Esgair-hir* there were around 500 miners, many of whom had come from Cornwall, and others who had been sent by force of law (for it was to the mines of Ceredigion (Cardiganshire) that they first started transporting criminals in this Kingdom) who before long made the place somewhat unruly. At that time a market was held at Esgair-hir, and these wicked men took possessions and stole from the market without paying if they did not get items for the price they demanded. The people of the country complained a great deal because of the unfit conduct of the miners, and the *"Children of the Garsiwn"* heard this, and decided to investigate the situation. Four of them went there; one from the Ffridd, on the other side of Pont-ar-Ddyfi, another from Maes-y-culyn, another from Cwm-y-rhaiadr, and the other from Ceniarth, armed with two sticks each – a short one for defence, and a long one for striking. They saw the habitual wrongdoers among the miners, and despite warning them intensively they did not cease. As a result, they started hitting them and hitting them, and they did so until they all fled for their lives to their holes, and the giants returned having achieved complete victory, and the welcome when they came to their friends in the "Garsiwn" was not small.

---

* It is interesting to note that in George Borrow's *Wild Wales,* written at around the same time, he refers to this mine as *Esgyrn Hirion,* or *Long Bones.* 'Esgair Hir' means 'long ridge' whereas *esgyrn hirion* means *long bones* (NIDF)

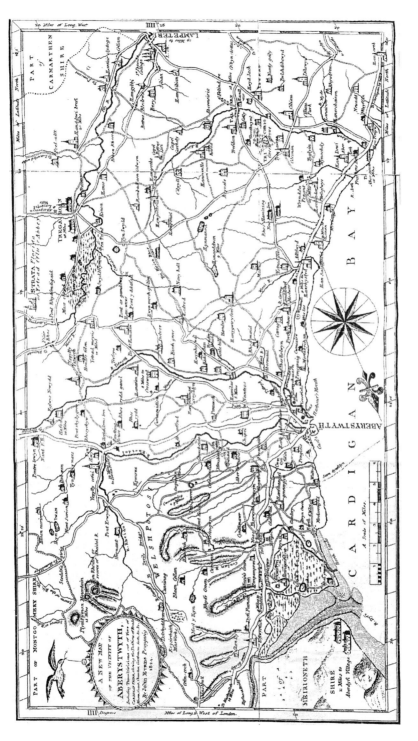

John Evans' 1824 map of Cardiganshire, showing what was then an important 'road' from Glaspwll to Devil's Bridge (now just a pathway), via the 'Welsh Potosi' in which Esgair Hir and Esgair Fraith lead mines were located

LLANEGRYN

A parish in the hundred of Tal-y-bont, 5 miles long, and 2 wide, consisting of around ten thousand acres of land, most of which is mountainous. The village stands near the River Dysynwy*. Around a mile from it is the church of the parish, which is dedicated to Saint Egryn ap Gwrydrdrwm ap Gwedrawg ap Geraint ap Garanawc ap Gwleddigar ap Cynwal ap Rychwin from Rhychwin in Rhos, from whom the name of the parish also comes.

The surrounding area is amongst the most beautiful and most pleasant ever seen – its small hills open to receive the visit of the sunshine, and small farms are scattered everywhere. The small, green, fruitful fields adorn it like a garden paradise, and crowning it all there appears some peaceful serenity completely commanding the whole.

In the parish is the farmhouse of Tal-y-bont, which was the residence of some of the Princes of Gwynedd, and a charter to Prince Llewelyn was dated in this place. A little away from the house is an earthwork of considerable curiosity, on which, it seems, was a watch tower associated with the mansion, and on the opposite side of the river, in the parish of Tywyn, there is a similar mound.

LLANFIHANGEL-Y-PENNANT

The meaning of the name Llanfihangel-y-Pennant is *"Church of Mihangel at the head of the valley or stream"*. This parish stands in the hundred of Ystumaner, in a narrow valley near the foot of the high mountain of Cader Idris, 12 miles from Machynlleth.

The parish is around 4 miles in length and three wide, and comprises a wide variety of land. The part of it which is valley-land

---

* Dysynwy = Dysynni (NIDF)

is exquisitely fertile, and noted for producing corn, while the mountainous part serves only to graze sheep.

The benefice here is perpetual Curate in the Archdeaconry of Merioneth, in the Diocese of Bangor; the church, as aforementioned, is dedicated to Saint Michael. The Independents also have a house of worship here. The village of Llanfihangel is only small, and its situation is pleasant on the bank of the River Dysynwy. The parish includes the tithe-towns of Llanllwyden and Maestrefnant.

As we leave the vale of Dysynwy, and follow the rivulet that discharges into that river nearby, we come to the remains of an old castle, which stands on a high rock, and is commonly called Teberri Castle, or Castell Cae'r Berllan*. In relation to the origins of the name there are many different opinions. Ieuan Brydydd Hir argued that the true name was *Castell yr Aberau*; another origin given to it is *Castell y Beri* (Castle of the Kites), as it is the haunt of a large number of birds of prey, some of which build their nests in the rock. Others suppose that it should be written *Castell y Bera,* and that it derives from the shape of the rock, which is not dissimilar to a hayrick or pyramid. I let the reader take his own pick of these meanings. Pennant thinks that this is the Teberri Castle associated with the Prince *'Llewelyn our last leader'*. And Thomas Walshingham says that William de Valence, the Earl of Pemboke, took it from the garrison after Llewelyn's death. It was visited by John I, and the *Ville de Bere* was deemed important enough to be given a charter by him. It is also likely that it was this castle that John bestowed into the care of Robert Fitzwalter, who was given the right to hunt every type of wild animal in this part of the land.

It is worth noting that another fortress of the same name exists in Ceredigion† (Cardiganshire). Despite this, not many years after the

---

* Now commonly called *Castell y Bere* (NIDF)
† Routiae Walliae, page 99

subordination of Wales, it seems it stopped being kept as a Royal fortress, if anyone lived there at all; for it is not alluded to except in a list of accounts for Meirionnydd (Merioneth) in the first year of the reign of Henry IV.

From the history we get from the ancient scripts of Hengwrt, from the time of the reign of Elizabeth, it appears that at that time it was almost as ruined as it is at present.

The castle hides the entire summit, and it was a place of great strength. The most complete room was 36 feet wide, and was cut on two sides from the rock*. The castle, and the rock on which it stands, were completely covered by trees and shrubs until 1850, when W. W. E. Wynne Esq., MP, cleared away the rubbish and undertook an investigation in the midst of the ruins. Nothing indicated the genre of the building, nor was there the least grain of old carvings to be found. This unearthing had, in any case, only just started when it became clear that it would prove to be very interesting; and the results prove that Castell Teberri was one of the biggest castles in North Wales, bearing in mind that the castles of Caernarfon and Beaumaris are exceptions; and that its building quality excelled them all. It stretches along the crest of the rock for more than 500 feet in length, and more than 150 feet in breadth†.

In this parish, in a smallholding called Ty'nybryn, on the 7th of August 1759, the profound scholar, ingenious historian, and magnificent linguist William Owen Pugh DCL, FAS, was born, author of the English and Welsh dictionary, which the learned of greatest fame, versed in both languages, and in several others, declare as being one of the greatest unrivalled masterpieces completed by one author in any language. It contains over ONE HUNDRED THOUSAND words which is close to the amount in the

* Pennant's Tour through Wales, Vol. ii, page 103
† Morgan's Guide to Aberdovey, page 112

generality of English dictionaries!

> *Os bywlawn Nicholas Baily – Eiriadur,*
> *A Sheridan eilfri,*
> *Johnson ben, mae'n OWEN ni*
> *A'r y gwŷr yn rhagori*

> *If Nicholas Baily of the Dictionary be sprightly,*
> *And Sheridan of the same renown,*
> *Johnson be chief, our OWEN*
> *Excels on all these men.²*

But despite its being a heavy task composing such a dictionary, and the time it was in his hands, it only made up a small part of Dr Pugh's labours. The periodicals were full, and the land chequered with his songs, essays, letters, etc; but the books he had the greatest hand in publishing were *Meditations on the Archaeology of Wales,* three octavo volumes; The Bardic Works of Dafydd ab Gwilym; The Work of Llywarch Hen, as well as a translation of the same to English; *The Cambrian Register,* three octavo volumes; The Cambrian Biography, the records of famous people amidst the Britons; Devotion of the Christian; an essay on farming; The Loss of Paradise, etc.. It would be to no avail to try and make any notes of his works, as they are so well known. He died suddenly at the age of 76 years, on a visit to his area of birth, in a place called Dolyddcae, Tal-y-llyn parish, on June the 3rd 1835.

LLANWRIN[*]

A parish in the hundred of Cyfeiliog, 4 miles to the northeast of Machynlleth. It stands at the most westerly part of the county of Trefaldwyn (Montgomeryshire), and is the only part beyond the River Dyfi. It includes a variety of meadow and mountain-land. The surrounding views are numerous and pretty, and from the highlands a glimpse can be had of the main mountains of North Wales, as well as most of the excellent vale of Dyfi, through which that crystal river makes its way.

It includes the tithe-townships of Llanfechan, Blaenglesyrch, and Glyncaerig. It is thought that the mountainous parts are full of mineral veins. Peat is dug there, which is used on the fires of most of the inhabitants.

The village of Llanwrin stands in a hollow under the side of a small hill, facing the Dyfi valley. It includes lots of houses, but little industry is carried out here, and that in relationship to nothing in particular.

Here stands the church of the parish, which is dedicated to Saint Gwrin. It is a sturdy building constructed in the early English fashion, 163 feet long. It is said in the *"Pedigree of the Saints"* that there were two Saints of the island of Britain, namely Ust and Dyfnig, residing in Llanwrin, who came here from Brittany with Saint Cadfan, who made his home in Tywyn, Meirionnydd (Merioneth).

The current incumbent is the Reverend I. Bonsall, who possesses an extensive collection of Greek, Roman, British and Irish minted pieces, as well as monks' seals from Ystrad Fflur (Strata Florida), and a wide variety of minerals.

There is a Calvinistic Methodist chapel here, and Capel Seion, a

---

[*] In the Myfyrian Archaeology it is called the "Wirin"

chapel associated with the same denomination, is a little higher up, in a small valley. The Independents also have a chapel nearby. Mrs Ann Pugh donated £50, an unknown benefactor £49, and Mr John David Evan £10, the interest from which, as well as that on numerous smaller gifts, are to be shared annually between the poor of the parish.

LLYFNANT

Around 6 miles from Machynlleth, amidst the mountains that lie between Plumlummon, is Llyn Penrhaiadr, from which runs the beautiful River Llyfnant.

This lake teems with fish, that, so say the old people, were taken from Rome when our country was in the possession of the Romans. The lake belongs to Pryse Loveden Esq., MP, who keeps careful observation of it.

In terms of the meaning of the name Llyfnant, some insist that it is *Llew-nant (Lion stream)* that should be seen (See GARREG); but it is very likely that *Llefn-nant* or smooth stream is the correct wording, despite its surface not being particularly smooth.

In order to get a full view of the magnificent glade through which the river flows, the best approach is to start at the bottom near the main road that leads from Machynlleth to Aberystwyth, 4 miles from the former place. From here a ride up along the valley can be seen, and one of the most beautiful scenes in Wales can be enjoyed for six miles, until the way is barred by a magnificent rock, over which the river pours as a terrible torrent, called Pistyll-y-llyn. Close to the source of this river is Cwm-y-Rhaiadr, and it is said that the Romans had a mine working here, which continues to the present.

MALLWYD

A parish belonging to the hundred of Cyfeiliog, although most of it is in the hundred of Talybont and Mawddwy, around 12 miles from Machynlleth. The meaning of the name is *Maen-Llwyd* (*Grey-Stone*), which it is assumed derives from a memorial pillar that formerly existed here, of which there are no remains.

The parish is broad, and includes an extensive share of arable land and grazing, under good cultivation, as well as a large portion of open, uncultivated land.

The position of the village of Mallwyd is beautiful, in a small but fruitful valley, with the high mountains of the Aran, Camlan*, and Moeldyfi surrounding it like an amphitheatre, and as if in competition with each other as to which can separate its head highest above the firmament to defend against the sally of the tempests.

The views on every side are diverse and picturesque, and include a multitude of objects of mixed beauty and portions of wild wilderness, amidst which are numerous pretty waterfalls in a variety of parts of the valley, such as by Pennantigi; another in the valley of Maesglasau; and another near Pont Mallwyd. The latter is near the village, and is formed by the labour of the River Dyfi flowing through a narrow, rocky bed, against a high rock in its middle, then pouring with great din to a pool below, while on the other side, near this place, the mountains of Camlan rise in wild majesty, with the bridge at their foot, enveloped in ivy which throws its claw-like strands over the terrible precipice.

Near this bridge, on the lower side, in the middle of the woods, on the side of the road that leads to Aberangell, is the small chapel of

---

* Camlan is said to be the site of the battle between Arthur and his nephew Medrawd. Various sources describe Arthur either dying during the battle, or being taken away to *Ynys Afallon* (NIDF)

101

Camlan, belonging to the Calvinistic Methodists. A few yards above there is also a house, with an opening associated with it, and a dam across the river to turn the fish into it.

The main road leading to Welshpool and Dolgellau runs through the village, and travellers and visitors can get comfortable and convenient rest in the clean hostel of the Peniarth Arms, which is kept by Mr E. D. Rowlands. It is a notable fact that this house is built partly in Meirionnydd (Merioneth) and partly in Sir Drefaldwyn (Montgomeryshire). The aforenamed gentleman, in association with the owners of several hostels, runs one carriage through the year, and two through the summer, between Croesoswallt (Oswestry) and Aberystwyth. This venture deserves the warmest support on account of the convenience it affords to travellers. It is not possible to find a road so full of natural beauty than the route of this carriage. It runs from Aberystwyth through the midst of rich scenery to Machynlleth; from there along the side of the watery valley of the Dyfi up to Mallwyd. At this place it leaves the Dyfi, and turns up to go over the bare brow of Bwlch-y-fedwen, where a rich, expansive area of Powys opens up ahead. It reaches Canoffice, and, having waited a minute or two there, it starts again, and after passing the large farm of Llysyn, which is a tithe-township in itself, and through Llanerfyl, a little higher up than this it leaves the Welshpool road, and turns towards the pretty vale of Meifod, passing through fertile cultivated lands, until it reaches the large and orderly village of that name. Going on from there, the traveller is entertained by the charming beauty of the wooded surroundings, until coming to Llansantffraid – and the interest does not at all cease while going from there onwards through the area of Porthywaen, until at last reaching Croesoswallt (Oswestry) and the coach-line for Amwythig (Shrewsbury), Caer-lleon (Chester), etc.

In the village of Mallwyd stands the parish church, built on the borders of two counties, and dedicated to Saint Tydecho, in which remains of great antiquity can be seen. The bell-tower, which is made mostly from wood, and was built in 1640, has the Latin words *Venite Cantem* (come and we shall sing) carved on it. Above the porch that leads into it hang the bones of a whale; this, so tradition has it, was caught in the River Dyfi! Also, inside the church is met something the like of which is apparently not seen in the Kingdom; namely that the altar stands in the middle. It was placed there by Dr Davies, and Archbishop Laud ordered that it be moved to the eastern side, as is usual; but the Doctor, despite the worst of the Archbishop, moved it back to the centre, where it remains to this day.

A great number of legends are recounted about Saint Tydecho, to whom the church is dedicated. *"Saint Tydecho's abilities to accomplish miracles"* said the Papists *"is not one bit less than those possessed by Narcipus II, the Bishop of Jerusalem, who, it is said, turned the water to oil to light the lamps of the church"* - Bacon[*].

Dafydd Llwyd ab Llewellyn ab Gruffydd, the Lord of Mathafarn, recounted the following about him: Tydecho was an Abbot in Armorica, or Brittany, and came over here at the time of King Arthur. But after the death of this leader, and the Saxons overrunning most of the Kingdom, the Saint retreated to the Mallwyd area, where he led the most severe life; he lay on the bare rocks, and wore a shirt of horsehair. Despite this, he used his time for good purposes, such as to till land, and in obliging and generous practices.

The Prince Maelgwyn Gwynedd, at that time just a youth, went and took possession of the Saint's oxen, and took them away from the yoke. The next day wild deer were seen fulfilling the role of the oxen, and a great grey wolf harrowing behind them. Maelgwyn, in irate

---

[*] Pugh's Cambria Depicta, page 197

rage at seeing this, took out his milk-white dogs to punish the deer, and he himself sat on a lump of rock nearby, to enjoy the excitement. But when he attempted to rise, he found himself inseparable from the rock, and he had to appeal for the forgiveness of the Saint, who, having received sufficient repayment, saw fit his release from his disagreeable bondage.

It is not unlikely that he succeeded in securing from Maelgwyn the granting, to this and other churches associated with him, special extra privileges, such as defensive sanctuary to man and beast, such that every criminal, no matter how guilty, could be sure of safety there. His lands were supposed to be free from all fighting, burning, and killing, and all ecclesiastical payments.

This place is highly honoured due to the famous Dr John Davies having ministered here. He was the son of Dafydd ab Sion ab Rhys, a weaver from Llanferes, Denbighshire. He was born here in the year 1570, and received part of his education in Oxford, where he gained the degree of Batchelor of the Arts. After that, in 1608, he moved to Lincoln College, and in 1616 received the degree of Doctor of Theology. In the meantime, he held numerous ecclesiastical positions.

Through the patronage of King James he received the incumbency of Mallwyd in 1604, as well as the Canonship of Llanelwy. He changed this for the prebendary* of Llannefyd. He also held the incomes from Llanymawddwy and Darowen, which was exchanged for Llanfawr near Bala, and some say that he also had the income from Garthbeibo.

He was of great assistance to Dr Parry in the revision of the Welsh Bible, namely the 1620 edition. In 1621 he published *A Latin Grammar of the Welsh Language* in which he demonstrated not

---

* A prebendary is a type of canon who has a role in the administration of a cathedral. When attending cathedral services, prebendaries sit in seats known as Prebendal stalls, which are usually located at the back of the choir stalls (NIDF)

only the extent of his knowledge of the constituents of the language, but also that he was exceedingly familiar with the work of those who had written in it. In his introduction, it states that he studied the language in detail over more than 30 years of his life.

However, in the year 1632, he published his main *magnum opus*[*], namely the Welsh and Latin Dictionary. In the same year he published his translation of a book called *Resolution*; and he was the translator, publisher, or editor of numerous other small books. Some say that it was he who translated the *"Articles of the Church of England"* into Welsh, but this claim is short on proof.

Dr Davies was very loving amidst his compatriots, and his memory was long respected by everyone who knew him. The parish of Darowen had a particular reason to remember him, because of his consideration towards them. He built most of the church, the bell-tower, and the parsonage. He also built numerous bridges in the parish; and on Bont-y-cleifion, near the village, the letters J D are shown in white stones, and the time it was built, namely 1640. Recently a new bridge was built a little away from it, but the old one was kept in respectful memory of its builder.

Dr Davies died on May the 15th 1644, and was buried in the chancel of Mallwyd church; and on his gravestone the following inscription is carved, which has, in parts, been worn away since many a year:

JOHANNES DAVIES, S.T.D.
RECTOR ECCLESLÆ PAROCHIALIS DE MALLWYD,
OBIIT 15 DIE MAJI,
ET SEPULTUS FUIT 19, A.D. 1644, IN VIRTUTIS,
POTIUS QUAM NOMINIS MEMORIA.

Which means:

---

[*] Magnus opus = great work (NIDF)

John Davies, sacred ecclesiastical luminary.
Incumbent of the parish Church of Mallwyd,
who died on the 15th of May,
and was buried on the 19th, A.D. 1644.
More memorable for his virtue than for his name.

It was in the parish that the terrible rabble called "Gwylliaid Mawddwy"* resided, and it is beyond question to us that readers will not begrudge us relating some of their history here.

Around the middle of the sixteenth century a band of villains formed in the neighbourhood of Dinas Mawddwy, who were given the above name, and soon they accumulated many more of a similar tendency from different part of the Kingdom, until they became a horde so numerous and despoiling that their dread was felt throughout the whole populace, and many inhabitants left the area in fear; for apart from despoiling wayfarers travelling on that road, they placed large tribute on the heirdoms of the gentlemen of the area, and if those did not pay anything, the Gwylliaid would stampede their animals in broad daylight, taking them away in droves to the woods and mountains near Dinas Mawddwy.

After their behaviour had grown to such insolence, a complaint was made to the government, and Royal authority was obtained to destroy them. This authority was entrusted to Sir John Wynn ab Meredydd, from Gwydir†, and Lewis Owen Esq., from Llwyn, near Dolgellau, who, in the meantime, had been made the Under-chamberlain of Gwynedd, and one of the Barons of the Welsh Treasury.

The two gentlemen gathered together an army of men for the purpose, and on Christmas eve, 1554, they succeeded, after tireless

---

* Gwylliaid Mawddwy = the Mawddwy Brigands. These are more commonly known nowadays as the *Gwylliaid Cochion = the Red Brigands,* due to the said prevalence of red hair amongst the members (NIDF)
†Gwydir, Conwy Valley (NIDF)

effort, in taking around one-hundred of the brigands into custody, and without right or trial they were executed without delay by hanging them on the spot, as was allowed by the authority given to them by the government.

Despite all this, there were many of the aforementioned despoilers who had not been subdued, and after these circumstances they were made more brutal than before, and decided amongst themselves to avenge the blood of their associates on the named gentlemen. And as it happened, because the aforesaid Lewis Owen was the High Sheriff of Meirionnydd (Merioneth), his official duties demanded that he go to the assize* held in Trefaldwyn (Montgomery), and, upon his return, preconceived treason was committed, and he was plotted against and betrayed by a swarm of these bandits, who knew that the Sheriff would come home through the edge of the parish of Mallwyd, and they exacted their treason in a narrow wooded valley in that neighbourhood, in a place called "Dugoed". There they cut down many trees, setting them as a barrier across the road to prevent the traveller's exit.

When Mr Owen came to that place, an arrow was shot at him which, so tradition has it, went through his head, such that he fell dead on the spot. And on this occasion, to show their brutality even more heinously, tradition recounts the following story:

There was a young man amongst those executed on Christmas Eve, as alluded to, and his mother pleaded most insistently with the Baron to save his life. When she was denied her request she bared her bosom crying out *"These breasts nurtured the men that will avenge the blood of my son by washing their hands in the blood of*

---

* Assizes were courts held to hear serious cases that could not be dealt with by the Quarter Sessions (local county courts held quarterly). The Assizes and Quarter Sessions were abolished by the Courts Act 1971 and replaced by Crown Courts (NIDF)

his murderer". So these men, after committing their treason against Mr Owen, as reported, went away, leaving their enemy there. But before going far they recalled their mother's vow, and returned to complete it literally; stabbing the body with their swords, they actively washed their hands in the blood of the Baron's heart.

Among Mr Lewis Owen's escort on his journey were six or seven of his neighbours, and amongst them was his relative, John Llwyd, of Ceiswyn, in the parish of Tal-y-llyn. He was spared by the brigands, who said to him *"You walk away, lean Llwyd"*. The reason behind this favour, it is said, was that Llwyd had shown considerable companionship to one of the brigands, having taken him to numerous places to show his notable speed as a runner.

It is also recorded that the chief men amongst the brigands were the owners of extensive property in the area; no less than eighty hearths. The position of their residence can be seen to this day on the upper edge of Dugoed-mawr smallholding. However, the entire inheritance of the different branches of the brotherhood went in forfeit to the Crown, except one smallholding, Digoed-isaf, the owner of which, although related to the others, it seems likely possessed more wisdom or honesty than the others. This smallholding was sold to the late Sir Watkin Williams Wynn around 80 years ago.

So much was the dread in this community of the devastation of the bandits that they were afraid of them coming into houses through the chimneys, and to prevent this old scythes and other arms were placed in them, secured solidly in the walls; such were to be seen in the chimneys of Dugoed-mawr up until fifty years ago, when they were removed*. The place where Baron Owen was killed is also indicated to this day by the name "Llidiard [Croes] y Barwn"†‡

---

* A number of old houses in the surrounding parishes are said to retain such deterrents in their chimneys (NIDF)
† Gwladgarwr, vol. vi, page 161
‡ Llidiard [Croes] y Barwn = The Gate [Cross] of the Baron (NIDF)

MATHAFARN

This respectable farmhouse stands on the northern side of the River Dyfi. It has been notable through the ages. It is thought that the name derives from Mathaern ap Brychan Brycheiniog, who is buried in Ceredigion* (Cardiganshire), and who doubtless resided either here or in the neighbourhood.

The bard and visionary Dafydd Llwyd ab Llewelyn ab Gruffydd, who flourished from 1470 to 1490 in this part of the Principality, lived here. Earl Richmond, later to become Henry VII, stayed one night here with the bard on his journey from Fishguard to Bosworth field, and, quite anxious to know his destiny in advance, intensively interrogated the visionary about his fate. Dafydd prudently answered that he could not answer a question of such gravity in a minute, and that he would give his opinion in the morning.

His wife, perceiving his great gloom, asked him the reason for this. He stated his problem to her, and she was surprised at his tentativeness, and said to him *"Why are you so simple? Prophesise well to him. If he is victorious then your character will be established, and you will succeed in honour and gifts; but if you are unsuccessful, there is no danger he will come back to take revenge on you"*. Dafydd gladly accepted this counsel, and the venture gave weight to the old Welsh proverb *"The counsel of a wife without asking"*.[†]

During the Civil War at the time of Charles I, the Commonwealth mobilised and subdued this part of the country, and attacked Mathafarn, the resident of which was Lewis Pugh Esq., who was loyal to the King, burning it to its foundations. But the old

---

* "Bonedd y Saint", Hanes Cymru by Carnhuanawc, page 190
† Local tradition also has it that Henry's response to Dafydd's prophesy was *"you will not then mind me taking all your horses, as you know they will be returned"* (NIDF)

gentleman, perceiving the infuriated rabble approaching, fled away. As he was running along the road up towards the valley of Glyncaerig, he reached the Pandy, which is now a woollen works, and the old fuller, who was at the time putting wool on the tenter*, seeing his haste, shouted at him, asking what the reason was for his appearance of haste and fright. He referred his attention towards the irate soldiers who were pursuing him. *"Lie down here"* he said. The old Welshman lay down and in a minute was covered by the flannels. With this the soldiers came by, and asked the old fuller whether he had seen Lewis Pugh running past. *"Yes"* was the answer; *"He has just gone out of sight over there: you deal with him quickly"*. Away they went at full gallop until they had gone far enough, and the old gentleman had enough time to escape.

Near Mathafarn is a piece of land known by the name of *"Cae'r Ywen"* (field of the yew) because an old yew tree grew there a long time ago, but which has, by now, been totally destroyed. There was also a stone road leading from this place to Mathafarn, but the hand of the workers has long since tilled this. However, the following tradition regarding it has been passed down from age to age, and we cannot not give it a place here:

> *Pan dramwych Ffridd yr Ywen,*
> *Lle mae Tylwyth Têg yn rhodien,*
> *Dos yn mlaen, a gwylia sefyll,*
> *Gwylia'th droed rhag dawnsfa'r ellyll*
>
> *When you travel along Ffridd yr Ywen,*
> *Where the fair folk walk,*
> *Hurry on, and watch you don't stand,*

---

* Stretching flannel on a frame, known as a *tenter,* the flannel being held onto the frame by *tenterhooks,* hence the saying 'on tenterhooks' (NIDF)

Watch your foot lest the dancing place of the elf

Two of Mr Pugh Mathafarn's servants went to work in Cae'r Ywen, and early in the afternoon the whole area was enveloped by such a murk of thick mist that the lads supposed that night had come. But when they came to the centre of the field they were lit up, and the darkness looked as if it had been completely left behind; so, assuming it was too early to return home, they sat down and slept. When one of them awoke he was surprised to discover that there was no one there but himself. He was greatly mystified by the conduct of his companion, but decided in the end that he had taken the message he had heard him talking of during the day. He went home, and when they asked about his friend he told them he had gone to the house of the cobbler.

The following day came, and they made further enquiries about the missing servant's whereabouts, but nothing could be said of him. In the end he went to the *"wise man"*, which was quite usual at that time, who said to him:

> *"Go to where you and the lad slept – go there exactly a year after you lost him – on the same day of the year – and at the same time of day. But be careful not to go into the ring; stand on the edge of the blue-green circle you saw there, and the boy will come there to dance with a host of cobblers; and when he comes close to you take hold of him, and pull him out as soon as possible."*

He did as he was commanded to do, and snatched the lad out. He then asked him: *"Do you not need feeding?"* to which he answered *"No"* because he had the rest of his lunch in his *wallet,* or satchel, from before he went to sleep. The lost one asked *"Is it not the night, and time to go home?"* without realising that a year had gone past.

111

He looked completely like a skeleton, and as soon as he tried food, he became a dead corpse!

How much truth there is in this fable we would not take it upon ourselves to say; but it demonstrates the old superstitions and the darkness that was an entity amongst our forefathers, and the glorious work that the Gospel did in our midst, by sending its light to inform *"those who sat in the country and shadows of death"*, and to hunt the darkness of superstition from our land.

MOELEIDDEW

The highest mountain in the neighbourhood of Cemmaes, around two miles from the church. On its top there are the remains of a large camp. For whoever was camped there, the position was extremely convenient to identify every enemy movement from whatever direction. The highest ridge of the bare mountain embraces a variety of views of the surrounding areas for many miles. If the viewer stands with his face straight to the east, he will see only a terrific desert of dark mountains stretching endlessly, as if some furious explosion had uprooted all the mountains of the moon, and hurled them down, scattered, higgledy-piggledy, over the whole area.

Turn to the northeast, and there is Aran Fawddwy, sustaining its place of counsel in the sanctuary of the clouds, with the other mountains like a defensive escort, standing in silent reverence around it. Under those yonder green slopes, by the foot of Moel Benddyn, is hidden Dinas Mawddwy. Five miles lower down is the whole delightful plain of Cemmaes, and the numerous farms speckling its surface.

To the south, the wooded hills can be seen approaching each other as closely as is possible, as if to hold a conference over the Twymyn, which runs between them; but having to recede back gradually here and there to bring into view the neighbourhood of Llanbrynmair.

Directly to the west, the eye runs along the length of the vale of the Dyfi, until its course is suddenly halted by the rise of the Pen-y-ddol hill, by the opening of the gap of Pennal, which ends the view. But further on, over the ridge of that rise, the Irish Sea shines in the rays of the sun as its waves break on the beach of Aberdyfi.

NEWYDDFYNYDDOG

This hill stands in the tithe-township of Tirymyneich (Land of the monks), Llanbrynmair, on the south-easterly side of the parish.

On top of the hill are numerous mounds, or cairns, and it is presumed that they were erected for the religious services of the Druids, or perhaps for some purpose by the "Monks" who were in the "land". The largest of these circles are twenty-seven and twenty-four yards in diameter, and on higher land, near the same place, is another circle made of smaller stones, around nine yards in diameter, and some presume that, because its place is so prominent, it was a watchtower. Here there are also four large stones placed in the ground angularly, and called *"Lled croen yr ych"* (The width of the ox's hide). An old tradition amongst the inhabitants has it that two horned oxen cried out for each other, one from this mountain, and the other from Mynydd Cemmaes, and such was their longing for each other that they perished, and in memory of this heartbreaking fact the hide of one of them was stretched out, and these stones were placed, one at each corner of it. But it is apparent that this is just an unfounded fable; for why did they not raise a similar monument for the other ox? The astute and inquisitive historian Carnhuanawc[*] said that the bard Cynddelw wrote a few

---

[*] Hanes Cymru, page 570

lines to Hywel ap Iefaf, in gratitude for the gift of a bull he had from him. It included the word *fannawc*, which was translated by Owen Pugh as 'speckled' such as derives from *fine mark*. But it is thought that it derives from *ban [bannawc] (beacon)*, and that it means *horned*.

The lines start as follows:

> *Reutun am rotes Hywel,*
> *Reitiawc veiniawc vannawe vil;*
> *Keuaus gan dreth ortethol*
> *Tarw têg talgarth yn gwarthal.*
>
> *Hywel gave me a gift,*
> *A prized animal, slim and horned,*
> *I received from one so desirable his gratuity*
> *The fine bull of Talgarth as extra payment.*[2]

I shall let the learned make what they will of these lines. Because Cynddelw resided in Pentre-mawr farmhouse, in this parish, it is quite natural to assume that his cow, and the "bull", were once here, and that the cattle could easily have suffered some misfortune and perished, and the bard, in memory of the generous donor and the beautiful animal, erected this monument.

Stone circle on Newydd Fynyddog

PENEGOES

A parish in the hundred of Cyfeliog, reaching to within a mile of Machynlleth. Some say that the name derives from Egwest, one of the lesser Princes of Wales, who, so tradition has it, was killed near here, in a place named to this day Llawr-pen-egoes. Others think that the true meaning is Pen-y-groes (Top-of-the-cross), because there were some Catholic remains here.

Doubtless the parish church was once in the possession of the Catholics, because in the wall on its right hand side as you go in is a hole in a rock in which Holy Water was kept to make the sign of the Cross as they went to undertake their ceremonies.

The parish stretches from the small village of Pontfelingerig, near Machynlleth, to Rhyd-y-porthmyn on the Dylifau, but it is narrow in width. Most of it is wild mountain-land, although rich in lead and copper metals, while its lower part is fertile and pleasant, with the little River Crewi, which rises near Rhoswidol, running through it.

The population of the parish in 1851 was 928. The parish church, which stands in a pleasant flat area, on the side of the road that leads from Machynlleth to Amwythig (Shrewsbury), is long, narrow, and unadorned. Its outside is covered completely in ivy. In the graveyard there is a very large yew tree. The church is dedicated to Saint Cadfarch. Nearby is a convenient inn. A little below the main road is the parsonage, which is a very pretty building with fruitful gardens and very sheltering trees surrounding it. Away from the church, in a curve at the bottom of a small wooded hill, is the splendid mansion of Gallt-y-llan, the dwelling of E. Davies Esq., with the magnificent lower parts of Penegoes stretching in front of it. On the edge of the main road, a little closer to Machynlleth, is Cadfarch's Well, which has restored rest and healing to the joints of many, apart from just the author.

Mr David Williams, Gelligoch, made a stone wall around it at his own expense, but this is now in ruins, and it is a great pity that it is in such an impaired state, such that it is quite an exploit going to see it, because of the extent of its grimness. Around the river and this place, on top of a small hill, stands the farmhouse of Penrhosmawr, and when Bedos lived there, as Gwallter Mechain said of him *"Bedos is addressed (by Lewis Glyn Cothi) as a person possessing a princely fortune, and as one who was in the habit of giving sumptuous entertainments"*. Lewis Glyn Cothi said the following about him:

Brenin egin Penegoes,
Bid ar ei waith bedair oes.
Mwy yw ei gyfoeth na'r môr,
A deufwy na da Ifor.

*Datgan cerdd i Dianis**
Y fed medd fo o oed mis

The king of the descendants of Penegoes,
May his work last for four ages of the earth.
His has wealth more than the sea,
And twice as much as Ifor.

· · ·

Singing a poem for Dianis,
Drinking month-old mead.[2]

LEWIS GLYN COTHI

Around three quarters of a mile to the south of the church stands the village of Tai-newyddion[†], which includes many houses, but is somewhat lifeless. There are numerous small shops here, and chapels owned by the Independents, Wesleyans, and Calvinistic Methodists.

Here, in the year 1713, the renowned landscape painter Richard Wilson, BA, was born. He was the son of the late John Wilson, incumbent of this parish. We are told that Richard had a good early education, but that one of the first things he showed an aptitude towards was drawing pictures of different objects that attracted his attention, and before he came to use appropriate materials for this, he would char the ends of wicker in the fire, and with them would form his pictures on the walls of the house and its surrounding stone walls, which were mostly built of the flat slates of Pumlummon.

He won the attention of Sir George Wynne, his relation, who paid for him to go to London when he was 15; but as misfortune would have

---

[*] Dianis – his daughter
[†] Tai-newyddion is now commonly referred to as Penegoes

117

it, his tutor was clumsy in the art, which was a great disadvantage to the learning of our countryman. Nevertheless, by the time he was 35 years old he had achieved such fame that he was entrusted to paint a portrait of King George IV, who was at that time the Prince of Wales, and another of his brother, the Duke of York. These portraits were painted at the request of Dr Hayter, the Bishop of Norwich, who was the two Royal Princes' teacher.

But to nurture and cultivate his genius further he took a journey to Italy, where he became well acquainted with the illustrious Zuearèli, from Venice, who accepted and trained him greatly. At around this time he also became acquainted with Vernet, the French artist, who afterwards achieved such fame. Vernet one day went to visit Wilson in his studio and perceived one of the Welshman's unique portraits, which pleased him so much that he begged to own it, on the condition that he gave one of his best portraits in exchange for it. Wilson conceded easily to these terms, and Vernet took the picture and placed it in his gallery, using every opportunity he could to direct visitors' eyes towards it and take notice of it. When some gentlemen from England came in and praised his paintings, he answered instantly *"Don't speak of my pictures when you have a countryman so masterly in your own possession, namely Wilson, the artist of yonder picture"*.

After that, Wilson went to London to a spectacular residence in an honoured position, and tutored a host of young scholars who were sent to him from every corner. His works are dispersed over the whole Kingdom, and are considered prime ornaments in the residences of the nobles of the three provinces. But as is always the case, his excellence created slanderers, libellers, backbiters, and liars against him, to the detriment of his spirits and health. He died on May the 18th, 1782, aged 69 years old.

Mrs Hemans, the brilliant English bard[*], lived in Penegoes with her sister, the wife of the late incumbent Mr Hughes, who became notable for her musical expertise, and for setting music to her sister's poetical works.

PENNAL

A parish in the hundred of Ystumaner, Meirionnydd (Merioneth), that reaches to within less than a mile of the town of Machynlleth. It includes the tithe-townships of Cwmcadian, Pennal Uchaf, and Pennal Isaf, and the number of inhabitants in 1851 was 607.

Cathrall stated in his *"History of North Wales"* that the meaning of the name is Penael – peak, or brow of the hill. Lewis states in his *"Topographical Dictionary of Wales"* that the parish is of little eligibility in terms of agriculture, since its soil is poor and thin. But, with every respect to historical authorities, we reckon the author is astray in this matter; the neighbourhood is a fertile place, and it is a parish with a multitude of fruitful and level farms.

The village of Pennal stands in a broad agreeable plain surrounded by high bare hills, 4 miles from Machynlleth, on the side of a small river that flows from the nearby mountains, and around half a mile from the banks of the Dyfi. It includes several hundred good houses in scattered parcels without any main street. There is one convenient inn there[†], and numerous small shops, in one of which the post-office is kept. The parish church, which is dedicated to Saint Peter, stands here. This is an ancient building, built in part from the ruins

---

[*] Felicia Dorothea Hemans (Nee Browne) was a granddaughter of the Venetian consul in Liverpool, and the mother of Charles Isidore Hemans (1817–1876), an English antiquary (NIDF)

[†] The current inn, called the Riverside, was referred to as *Tŷ Brics* by previous generations due to the roman bricks used in its construction (NIDF)

of the old fortress of Cefncaer. It was pulled down in 1761 and rebuilt with the same materials.

The graveyard is very small, and is very full because one part of the parish of Tywyn bury their dead here, and it is so surrounded by the village such that there is no way to extend it. The income is in the perpetual curacy of the diocese of Bangor. There are also houses of worship here owned by the Calvinistic Methodists, Wesleyans, and Independents. Near the village is a large British School, which was built mostly through the means of Miss Thruston, Talgarth, who was extremely obliging to the poor of this place.

Woodward states in his *History of Wales* that a letter from Owain Glyndwr to the King of France was dated in this place. Many antiquities are associated with Pennal. Near the village is the farmhouse of Cefncaer, or the back of the fortress, which was a robust Roman camp at the time of the Emperor Honorius[*]. Mr Robert Vaughan of Hengwrt states that he saw a piece of silver with a Domitian[†] imprint on it dug from the earth near here. The old bell-ringer of Pennal also found primeval silver while planting potatoes in a field near the house. Tradition has it that an underground way reaches from this castle to Owain Glyndwr's house in Machynlleth[‡]. But some argue against this by saying that it would have been a way full of water because it crosses the Dyfi. But we see no weight in this reasoning, for our ancestors were not so bad at building work that they could not have made a tunnel under the River Dyfi. Furthermore, Ann Williams, an old woman from Pennal who is 84 years old, attests that the end of this way can be seen in the cellar of

---

[*] Cefn Caer house is where Owain Glyndwr is thought to have written the "Pennal Letter" of 1406. The Roman fort is now thought to be Flavian (1st Century AD). Honorius ruled in the 3rd Century AD (NIDF)

[†] Titus Flavius Domitianus, commonly known as Domitian, was the last emperor of the Flavian dynasty, who reigned from 81 AD until his death in 96 AD (NIDF)

[‡] Royal House, Machynlleth (NIDF)

Cefncaer, with the arch blocked up with stones. Another old woman called Margaret Jones, from this village, says that within living memory the arch was to be seen in the side of the lane to Cefncaer after quite a bit of rain. Another old woman from the village, called Betty Edward, says she saw the end of this underground way in Machynlleth when she was just a girl, and that she saw giant skulls that had been retrieved from it. The author can also testify to having heard a hollow sound in the ground after having struck his foot on the ground in numerous places on the lane to Cefncaer.

Throughout the area there is a tradition that a cauldron full of silver is hidden somewhere on the land of the holding of Cefncaer, and one reputable farmer from the neighbourhood was, years ago, foolish enough to give the sum of £20 to encourage speakers who would tell him where it was. Scoundrels pocketed the money, but there is no need to advertise the fact that the cauldron stayed hidden.

It is likely, says Cathrall, that a Roman road leads from Conovium (Caer Rhun, near Conwy), to Lucarum, near Swansea, which passed by Dolgellau, to the west of Cader Idris, on to Pennal, and from there passed the splendid mansion of Talgarth over to the Gareg, and on to Llanbadarn Fawr[*], where Roman remains have been found, and then through Llanfihangel-y-creuddyn, where there are proven remains of a Roman road; from there again to Llanino, six miles from Llanbedr-pont-stephan (Lampeter), where numerous Roman carvings have been discovered; from there over to Talley, Llandeilo Fawr, and Llwchwr.

A little below the village, near the bank of the Dyfi, is an artful

---

[*] The road linking the Roman forts at Pennal and Carmarthen is *Sarn Helen*, thought to be derived from Sarn y Lleng, which means road or causeway of the legion. In the mid 1970s aerial photography revealed the remains of one of the largest forts in western Wales at Penllwyn, Capel Bangor, some 3 miles to the east of Llanbadarn Fawr, on the course of what is almost certainly Sarn Helen.

mound, called *Tomen Las*, on top of which a fortress or castle was undoubtedly built to defend and watch the ford on the river. It is supposed by the inhabitants that Wtre Pennal, which leads to Felin-Parsel, was made up of graves, and it is said that bones have been found there; the result, it is thought, of some bloody battle fought there in ancient times – and in searching the pages of history we discover that this is not unfounded imagining: a hard battle was fought here between Thomas ab Gruffydd ab Nicholas from Dynefor, for the House of Lancaster, and Harri ab Gwilym from the court of Henry, one of Earl Pembroke's commanders, for the House of York, when Thomas ab Griffydd won the field. A bloody battle also took place here between the same Thomas ab Griffydd ab Nicholas and David Gough, a close relation of another Gough, a famous warrior in the reign of Henry V. ab Nicholas came victorious from this contest for a second time: David Gough fell under the edge of his sword. But despite all this it appears that he did not get to leave the area alive; for Lewis says of the large mound, or Domen-las, on the land of Talgarth, that it is a tumulus raised on the grave of Thomas ab Gruffydd, and some of his soldiers, who were killed by some of the other party in the glade while asleep.

In this village once lived the most loveable and beautiful of all the maidens of Gwynedd, Lucy Llwyd[*]. Her incredible and melancholic death, although quite favourable to her feelings, cannot do less than induce sympathy and compassion. She was in courtship with Llewelyn Goch ab Meurig from Nannau, a bard, but her father, in a passionate hour, and being displeased with the union, took advantage of the absence of her love in South Wales, and tried to break the attachment. With this intent, he told her that Llewelyn

---

[*] More normally referred to as *Lleucu Llwyd*, who is said to have been from Dolgelynen, a farm on the north bank of the Dyfi, between Machynlleth and Pennal (NIDF)

had left her and married another.

The blow was more than she could sustain; she fell down and died on the spot. Llewelyn, returning one or two days after this, hurried to his heart's beloved, and the sudden shock of seeing her placed in her coffin affected his senses so much that he fell down as dead on the floor. Despite this, he was resuscitated, and composed an elegy in which is portrayed, with the feelings of a forsaken man and a distraught mind, the character of the most exquisite among girls, in which he says the following:

Cefn Caer

123

Llyma haf llwm i hoew fardd,
Llyma haf llwm i fardd:
Nid oes yn Ngwynedd heddiw
Na Lloer, na llewyrch, na lliw;
Er pan rodded trwydded twrch
Dan lawr dygu, dyn loer degwch.

For blithe bard, barren summer,
And a barren world for a bard.
There is in Gwynedd today
No moon, no light, no colour,
Since was laid, sorry welcome,
Moon's beauty beneath hard ground.[3]

From the engraving on her tomb it appears that she died in 1402[*].
Near this place is Talgarth, a beautiful mansion on a small hill, in the middle of thick trees, in view of the whole of the Dyfi valley and the delightful district of Pennal, the residence, until recently, of the venerable Gadben Thruston, R. N., but currently that of his son, C. F. Thruston Esq.

A little to one side, up between the hills, is the new mansion of Trefanau, the current dwelling of Cadben Thruston, a large, beautiful building, which is exceedingly fine. On its western side is a type of tower, which is 21 yards in height. When it was in his sight, Lewis Glyn Dyfi sang the following about it:

---

[*] The fact that Llewelyn Goch died in 1390 suggests that this is an error. However, some have speculated that the poem about Lleuci Llwyd was symbolic, rather than autobiographical, as the name Lleuci Llwyd appears elsewhere in Welsh poetry. There is now no trace of such a tomb, and local historians are unaware of any reference, other than in this work, to its existence. However, Lleuci Llwyd is said locally to have been buried to the right of the altar in Pennal church (NIDF)

Tŷ Newydd o tan awel – y bryniau
A'r bronydd glas tawel;
Gan bob gŵr, gan bawb a'i gwel,
O'i achos rhoi'r clod uchel.

A new house under the hills' breeze
And the calm green slopes;
Every man, and every one who sees it,
As a consequence gives the highest praise.[2]

PENNANT

A tithe-township in the southwest of the parish of Llanbrynmair. It is a long narrow valley, with slopes of emerald beeches that make its slopes appear sublime. It was formerly called "*Pennant Bacho*", as seen in the lines of Lewis Glyn Cothi:

Ac yno tario hyd dydd,
Yn Mhennant Bacho beunydd

And there, tarry the length of the day,
In Pennant Bacho always.[2]

We cannot say from where it got its name.

Because of some resentment between Henry, King of England, and the Welsh Princes, it was decided that the name of the Welsh should be erased from the Earth, and with this intent a host of chosen soldiers was mustered, and they were dispatched into three sections, one being sent with Gilbert, a Prince from Cornwall, another with

125

Huw, the Earl of Caerleon, and Alexander, the son of Moel Cwlwm, and the third section he led himself. But the Welsh Princes transported their livestock to the mountains of Eryri (Snowdonia), and from there badgered the Royal army immensely. The army of Alexander and the Earl came to Pennant; but before doing any damage the parties found peace, and the army returned to England.

There is an orderly appearance to the farmhouses in this place, and the farms appear in good condition. The main landowner here was lately Sir John Conroy, who was so credit-worthy for his efforts on behalf of the agricultural industry amongst his tenants.

There is another valley called Cwm Crygnant running parallel with it, but with a ridge of mountain separating it, along which an *old road*, formerly a main road, leads to Llanidloes. In the furthest corner of Pennant a high mountain rises, and in this place the famous waterfall of "Ffrwd Fawr" pours, with stupendous din, forty-five yards in depth, over the terrible jagged rocks. Being close to it on one of February's tempestuous days gives quite an explanation of the words *"like the sound of many waters"*. Under the shelter of this stupendous rock, in a secluded nook, stands the small village of Cilcwm, and a little below it is Capel y Pennant, owned by the Calvinistic Methodists.

PONTFAEN

From Machynlleth we turn to the Llanidloes road, which goes past the place where fairs and races were formerly held, and having travelled around a mile and a half we are in Pontfaen, or *Y Fforge*.

The village is built on the banks of the River Dulas, and its houses are scattered and unadorned. There are four woollen works and one fulling mill here, and a broad range of industry is carried out here. In the lower part of the village, a stone bridge, which is almost completely covered in thick ivy, is thrown over the river. Away from the bridge is a large indentation in the rock, which is commonly called "Ogof Fathew", from the tradition that the ghost of some girl called Esther Matthews sometimes makes its appearance here – but I am confident that every such old superstition has by today completely vanished from our country.

The village is sometimes called "Fforge", and it is likely that there were formerly old furnaces here, to smelt iron, etc. – and there are several things related to the old works still here today, but I failed to get any clear information about it. The Calvinistic Methodists have a house of worship here.

A little closer to Machynlleth than this village, on the slope of a small hill, is a deep hole in the ground, full of water, and it is called "Ogof Wyddan". Tradition has it that it reaches an underground road from here to Dolguog, and this does not appear to be totally without foundation; for the traces of the old road can be found in several places, especially on the lump of hill next to Pontfelingerrig; and a similar hole, or cave, to the one alluded to is now visible near Dolguog. It is commonly thought that it was a mine works belonging to the Romans[*].

---

[*] Ogof Wyddan = Sorcerer's Cave. According to the 1856 *Cambrian Journal* "*an active miner, named Morris Williams, conceived this to be an old Roman mine-work, and applied for a take note from Sir Watkin W. Wynne, which being granted, he communicated his wish to make a trial to a Mr. Weston, a gentleman residing in the town; and he, having promised the necessary funds, the work commenced [in 1856] by getting the water out, which appeared to be about 16 feet. In their progress they came to the wood-work of a shaft, to the bottom of which a few days brought them. They then found a second shaft, also timbered, about 15 feet deeper, and having worked at this for a short time, without much progress, against the water, &c., there being obstructions and danger, it was deemed better to drive a level into the shaft*".

Ogof Wyddan (fenced off) with the site of the
Parc Common racetrack in the background

A number of artefacts including small 'celts', a short pick and a 'boulder stone...with a withy twisted round it for a handle' were recovered from the working before mining ceased sometime before 1869.

In 1996 the location of an ancient spoil mound was identified following the discovery of several stone mining tools within the outcast of a badger sett. The site was surveyed and excavated the following year and charcoal recovered from these layers was dated to between 1890 and 1630 BC. The cobbles used as hammer stones at the mine are largely of igneous origin, the nearest source for these being Tonfanau beach north of Tywyn. See *Timberlake, S & Mason, J, 1997, 'Ogof Wyddon (Machynlleth Park Copper Mine), Machynlleth', Archaeology in Wales 37, 62-5.* (NIDF)

Creigiau Rhosygarreg (Rhosygarreg Rocks), with Rhosygarreg farm in the foreground

PUMLUMMON

Amongst all the mountains of Wales there is not one that rises to the attention of the traveller more than Pumlummon; and there is not one, with the exception of Snowdon, that awakens in the breast of the Welshman as much historical interest. The meaning of the name is Pum-lluman (five banners/standards): those, it appears, that were raised on it to identify the camps of the old Welsh armies when they were camped on it. As its history is so important, and its breeze so wholesome, and such splendid views are to be enjoyed from its peak, it would not be inexpedient to take a trip to see it.

Leaving the main road that leads to Llanidloes, we turn to a path less travelled upon, which contracts greatly on the way to Rhosygareg, a mountain farm greatly noted for the abundance of hares that lurk throughout it. From here, we ascend the steep precipice of Cwmgwarchau, which, as the name indicates, was a place of siege for old warriors in former times. There is nothing particularly attractive in view until Rhosygareg has been passed, but here the magnificent nature fully repays the dreariness of the other part of the journey.

Below, a growling rivulet rushes over its rocky bed, taking into its bosom another stream; and the valley yields good crops of corn and hay. With the hideous and horrible Taren-y-bwlch-gwyn on the right, with a mountain-stream pouring to a depth of at least 250 feet, the naked moor of Llechwedd Cwmgwarchae is on the left, forming one of the most majestic views one can imagine.

After reaching the brow of the hill we go over a productive flat peat bog, part of which is called Mawnog Pen Llechwedd, and another part, Taren-gallt-y-cwm, from where, for the first time, we get a glimpse of the venerable mountain of Pumlummon. Before long we are on its peak*.

We perceive that the ridges of the mountain are three in number, Pumlummon Fawr, Pumlummon Is-llyn, and Pumlummon Fach, but that the three come under the same common name. The highest of these, namely Pumlummon Fawr, is 2463 feet above the surface of the sea. The height of Snowdon is 3571, and Cader Idris 2914. Pumlummon Fawr has two peaks, on each of which is a cairn. The one on the higher peak is similar to a pyramid, and is intended, it seems, as a place to put a warning beacon. Scattered around it are patches of coarse grass, blended with stacks of loose stones and bits

---

* This location is not close to the summit of Pumlummon, which is much further on (NIDF)

of rock, in the wildest mixture. From the highest ridge, which is regularly visited by a large variety of wild birds, a very broad view is had, including to the south the mountains of Ceredigion (Cardiganshire) and Maesyfed (Radnorshire); to the west the harbour of Aberdyfi and Saint George's Channel; to the north Cader Idris and some of the mountains of Eryri (Snowdonia); to the northeast the mountains of the Treiddyn near Trallwm (Welshpool); and, to the east, parts of the counties of Henffordd (Hereford) and Amwythig (Shrewsbury).

Pumlummon was the site of many bloody and warlike campaigns, and the numerous cairns that cover its ridges are now testament to how bloody and often the aforementioned must have been. There are three of these on it, and it is said they include stones laid, one upon the other, to denote the resting places of some of those who fell prey to the sword; and they also served as lookout towers. It was customary in times gone by for everyone who went past these cairns to add a stone to the pile.

The continual feuds between Owain Cyfeiliog, Prince of Powys, and Hywel ap Cadwgan, were worked out on this mountain.

Here also the immortal warrior Owain Glyndwr made his camp while attempting to reclaim the Royal Crown into the midst of the Gwalia aristocracy. In the breast of the mountain lies Hyddgnant*, where our hero fought the most Herculean charge in his lifetime.

> *"Because Owain knew well that the Flemish who had settled in Dyfed and Ceredigion were faithful tenants to the benefactors, the Kings of England, he badgered them somewhat severely, making regular attacks into their territories from his high camp until they decided at last to have a fair try at putting an end to him and his forays. So,*

---

* Now known as *Hyddgen* (NIDF)

having mustered around fifteen-hundred armed men, they surrounded him and part of his army on the mountain of Hyddgnant, such that things were very tight for him. But he inspired the few men who were willing to sell their lives at the greatest expense they could, even though they were merely two or three hundred men. And so they broke their way through the ranks, leaving over two-hundred men dead on the field, and driving the rest in flight, as if attacked by a troop of ghouls."[*]

Pumlimmon, with Glaslyn in the foreground

[*] "Darlithiau ar Hanes y Cymry" by O. Jones, page 243

This mountain also attracts considerably large attention because the Rivers *"Severn, Wye, delightful in their complexion, and Rheidol great its honour"* originate on it, the former being the longest in the Kingdom, and second only to the Tafwys (Thames) in terms of industrial importance, while the Rheidol and Gwy (Wye)   run through pleasant and beautiful scenery.

RHIWSAESON

A tithe-township in the northeast part of the parish of Llanbrynmair. It is a long, narrow valley that runs through the high mountains, with the road leading from the Wynnstay Arms along the bank of a pretty river. A little further up the valley is the village of Pandy Rhiwsaeson, which includes a multitude of houses and a house of worship owned by the Independents. A little above this village is the ancient farmhouse of Rhiwsaeson, which, it seems, gives the area its name. The traveller is led to it through very ancient trees which enshroud the access on all sides. It was once the honourable residence of a long lineage of the dignified Owen family*.

On the top of a high hill nearby are the remains of an old house, and it is assumed that this was a summerhouse owned by the family. One of these Owens was a lawyer, who had his office in the village of Pandy, and the stone road led to it from this place.

A little further up is Cwm Clegernant, which includes a multitude of cultivated farms. The small River Cleger runs past, and before long is joined by Nant-y-carfan and numerous other streams; then by the

---

* Athelstan Owen of Rhiwsaeson married Ann Corbet, a descendent of Llywelyn ab Cynwrig ab Osbwrn, and Nest, daughter and heiress of Gruffydd ab Adda of Dôl Goch and Ynysmaengwyn. This link between the two estates can be seen in the identical designs of the barns at Ysguboriau, near Ynysmaengwyn, and Rhiwsaeson (NIDF)

Iaen, which originates on the outskirts of Carno. After a pleasant journey between fruitful meadows for a short way, it discharges into the Twymyn near Tafolwern.

RHYD-Y-FELIN

Or, as is seen sometimes, "Melinbyrhedyn", which is a village in a small valley in the parish of Darowen, with the River Crewi running through it. It includes many poor workers' houses, without any particular industry being carried out. There is a beautiful new house of worship owned by the Calvinistic Methodists here. The surrounding area is mountainous, but mostly under agricultural cultivation.

TAFOLWERN

Or Walwern, as some write the name; a tithe-township in the lower part of the parish of Llanbrynmair. The small village of the same name stands in the flat lowland on the banks of the River Twymyn, near the place where it joins another large river. It only includes a few houses, and these are not in the best state or of the best fabrication. There is a house of worship owned by the Independents and an excellent water mill in it. From the names given to different parts of this village, it appears that it was formerly larger and far more dignified than it presently is.

It is hailed as: *"The Walwern worthy of a magnificent street and the costly walled castle"*. Here Owain Cyfeiliog, son of Gruffydd ab Meredith, Prince of Powys, established his court, and it is extremely likely that he built the castle alluded to. In 1162 we are told that

Hywel ap Ieuaf ap Elystan Glodrydd, who was the Lord of some of the Welsh lands between the Wye and the Severn, came and attacked Tafolwern Castle while Owain was away from home, and, through deceit, occupied the castle. When Owain heard this he fretted immensely, and mustered a host to take against Hywel, and went as far as Llandinam, preying on and pillaging everything in his way. When the people of the land saw this they rallied to Hywel, with the intent of pursuing their enemy, and on the banks of the Severn there was a bloody battle between them in which two-thirds of Hywel's men were killed. Owain returned and repaired and fortified his castle. Near the confluence of the two aforementioned rivers is a high mound which the locals commonly call *"Tomen Fawr"*, and some presume that it was here that the castle stood. But we cannot agree with this; for, in our opinion, it is not large enough to form the base of a castle, and a hole was cut through it recently, but all that was found was small stones mixed with earth which would be incalculably too weak to form the footing of a secure castle. Perhaps, notwithstanding this, it was a type of defensive tower[*].

Owain Cyfeiliawc was one of the most courageous and able warriors of his time, and he was one of the most exquisite sons of the reign, as numerous of his compositions testify, especially the *"Hirlas"*. This song was composed with a view to the Royal drinking cup, which contains half a pint. It is commonly filled during feasts, and is taken around the guests by the cup-bearers. For lack of space we must leave it out here.

Giraldus says of Owain that *"he possesses more oratory skills than his fellow Princes, and is famous for keeping good order in his*

---

[*] Tomen Fawr is in fact certainly the location of Owain Cyfeliog's castle. It was later occupied by Owain Gwynedd and then his son, Gwenwynwyn. In 1244 Owain Gwynedd's grandson, Gruffydd, was besieged in the castle by a Welsh army, following his support for Henry III, and John le Strange wrote to the King asking for his help (NIDF)

territories". His *"family-bard was Cynddelw, who resided near Tafolwern in a place called Pentre-mawr"*.

A photograph of what is likely to have been the site of the southern gate to Tafolwern castle. The rivers Clegir and Twymyn are, respectively, to the right and left of the road. They then move apart before finally coming together some 500 feet downstream, creating a natural moat.

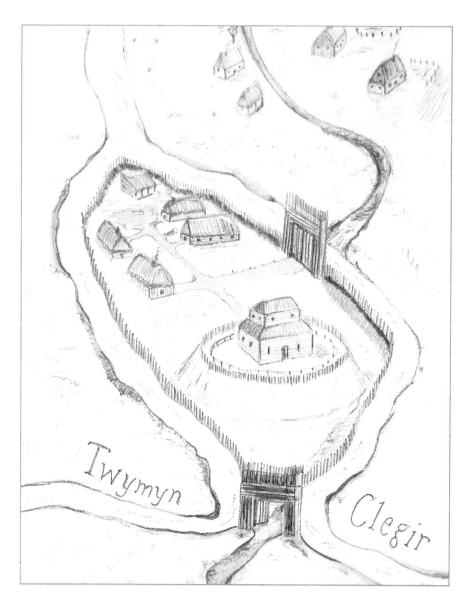

An impression of Tafolwern castle as it might have been, drawn by Elizabeth Fenwick, showing the southern entrance, and a ford close to the site of the modern bridge to the north.

TAL-Y-BONT

A long village, on quite a steep slope, either side of the main road that leads from Machynlleth to Aberystwyth, 11 miles from the former. A river flows below it, and there are a few houses on its other side. This place is becoming more popular and important daily because of the flourishing aspect of the mine workings in the nearby mountains. There are in it numerous shops and inns, and two large chapels owned by the Baptists and Independents.

TAL-Y-LLYN

This district lies by the foot of Cader Idris, on its smooth westerly side. The parish, which stretches over eight miles in length and four in breadth, takes into it a large part of the above wide-reaching mountain. It includes around thirty-six thousand acres of land, of which only around six thousand are cultivated, the rest being goat and sheep walks and pasture.

The name of the village derives from the fact that the position of the church is at the head of a beautiful lake, which is sometimes called Llyn Mwyngil, or Tal-y-llyn. There is only a little batch of poor houses, inferior in appearance; but regarding the area, it is answered in full in the portrait of the bard:

> Talyllyn, tawel le llonydd – iachus,
> I ochel ystormydd,
> Cysgodawl freiniawl fronydd,
> Gwempus oll, o gwmpas sydd.

> Lle destlus hoenus hynod – lle nodwych,
> Llawn adar a physgod;

138

Pob cysur eglur hyglod,
Anian bur, sydd yno'n bod.*

Talyllyn, quiet still place – wholesome,
To evade storms,
Sheltering, majestic hills,
All splendid, are all around it.

A tidy gleeful remarkable place – a notable place,
Full of birds and fish;
Every evident, illustrious comfort,
Pure quality, abides there.[2]

Most of the vale is covered by the lake, which lies pleasantly in its bed between the high mountains. There is an abundance of some of the fairest trout in the Principality in it, and freedom to enjoy unlimited use for the host of fishermen who visit the place for this purpose. When the water is low, the remains of a large cairn are visible, covering around an acre of land[†].

The lake is around a mile and a quarter in length, half a mile wide, and three in perimeter. Its owner is Sir Robert Vaughan from Hengwrt, and Rhug, near Corwen. It was bought from his uncle, the Colonel Vaughan, in order to give his friends the pleasure of fishing in it; but the poor and the rich, the stranger and local, are equally welcome to its use. There are also numerous small boats for the use of visitors. It covers so much of the vale that there is only a narrow place at either end of it, and the mountains reflect in its clear waters. On the south-westerly edge is the comfortable inn of Ty'nycornel, which is kept by Mr Evan Evans. From there, a full view of the

---

* "Diliau Meirion", page 129
[†] Parry's "Cambrian Mirror, Page 269

diverse beauty of the vale can be had. In the visitor's book kept by Mr Evans there are a host of commendatory testimonies to Mr Evans and his family for the fine attention paid to visitors, and the reasonable charges for the same. At the other end, on the northeast side of the lake, stands the ancient farmhouse of Dolffanog, which has been famous for many years as the residence of a branch of the Penygareg family. One bard says of this place as follows:

> *Yn min y llyn, mewn lle enwog – gwiwlwys,*
> *Y gwelir Dolffanog:*
> *Da odiaeth le godidog,*
> *Meithriangar i'r gerddgargog.*

> *Lle syniawl yw llys Owen, - mewn hirddol,*
> *Man harddaf dan wybren,*
> *Ei ddawnus barchus berchen,*
> *Heb wanhau fo byw yn hen*

> *On the edge of the lake, in a famous, worthy place,*
> *Dolffanog can be seen:*
> *And exquisitely, glorious place,*
> *Nurturing for the tuneful cuckoo.*

> *Owen's court is a contemplative place – in a long meadow,*
> *The prettiest place under the sky,*
> *May its gifted, respectable owner*
> *Grow old without weakening.*[2]

Tal-y-llyn

Away from Dolffanog is another part of the district called Ystradgwyn, which is flat, fertile land, chequered with small farms, none being far from the next. This plain was formerly open bare land, where the residents of this place and Corris would assemble together to play the male-sport of foot ball. Apparently, it was the Corrisians who would most often win the field, which excited one of them to declare his victorious exultation in the following old verse, which is still to be found in the memories of many throughout the area:

> *Ni wiw i 'Stragwyn gicio côl*
> *A phobl wrol Corris;*
> *Mae nerth yr uwd yn môn y glin*
> *Yn gwneud y dyn yn ddawnus.*

It is vain for 'Stragwyn to kick a goal*
With the brave people of Corris;
The strength of porridge in the base of the knee
Makes the man talented.

The Calvinistic Methodists have a chapel here. In the little smallholding in the middle of the woods, namely Dolyddean, the immortal Dr W O Pugh ended his earthly career. He came here by chance on a visit to his old area of birth; he went to rest the night before, healthy as usual, but by the morning he had had a visitation of dumb paralysis, and his soul had flown away.

Nature here is dressed at its wildest; the black rocks along the foothill of the Gadair testify that at some time they have been affected by fire. While climbing through the woods and shrubs, with the sides of the rugged cliffs along the edge of the rivulet that runs down to the vale, we come to Llyn Cau, nestled in its deep bed between the craggyness of the rocks, as if wishing to hide completely from view, to avoid attracting the attention of visitors away from its more honourable brother on the plain. It is around a quarter of a mile in length, and the same amount in width. Its appearance resembles the mouth of a volcano, which, along with the involuntary dread that arises in the viewer while standing on its edge under the heaped rocks, induce one to feel as if he were above the Tophet of the Israelites. A little higher up, the mountains almost meet, and their appearance is rugged and wild.

By starting from Min-ffordd, an inn by the road higher up from Dolffanog, the traveller goes ahead on the road that leads to Dolgellau, with the foot of the mountain, which is split into countless cliffs, hanging in a scowling poise above the valley below. One of these is called Penydelyn (Head of the harp), from its

---

* Ystradgwyn (NIDF)

resemblance to that instrument, and another by the name *"the parson and the sexton/bell-ringer"*, as it looks from afar as sinisterly similar to that as one can imagine. Also among them is a unique column of rock which, from a little away, appears exactly like a man standing on a cliff to look upon those who are passing by. On top of the Bwlch is a row of etched rocks called Llam-y-lladron (the thieves' leap), from which, tradition has it, they would formerly throw evil-doers, who would lose their lives in the fall, and disappear from sight in the lake at their foot, namely Llyn-tri-Graeryn, or, as it is sometimes called, Llyn Bach*. It received the former name from three giant rocks on its shore†; those that tradition has it are three pieces of gravel that the giant Idris felt irritating his feet, until it induced him to undo his shoes and shake them out in this place. The depth of the lake is unknown; it has not been found. Another extraordinary fact about it is that it is grey throughout the year; after three months of dryness in the middle of summer, its colour will still be the same as in the middle of the winter's rain.

In the valley below is the sparkling spring of Ffynon Rhwyfor. It is said that it is very effective in treating articular rheumatism and other ailments.

At the foot of the high mountain, a little below the village of Tal-y-llyn, stands the old and famous residence of Maes-y-pandy. It was formerly owned by a branch of the Nannau family. The last of these died in the year 1764. Its current owner is Nannau Wynn Esq., who has just come of age.

In this parish, in a place called Llwyn Dol Ithel, in the year 1684, around three yards deep in the earth, a wooden coffin was found, seven feet in length, carved and gilded at each end. Two skeletons were found in it, male and female, so it is assumed, the head of one alongside the feet of the other. The bones were dank and fragile and

---

* This lake was drained when the road was improved (NIDF)
† Llyn-tri-Graeryn = Lake of the three pieces of gravel (NIDF)

of giant proportions – the femurs being 27 inches in length.

Around the year 1570, Sir Owain ab Gwilym, a famous bard and a clergyman, held the curacy of this parish. It appears that he was very obliging to the bards, who poured out their melancholic feelings to him. William Lleyn produced an excellent elegy to him, which starts:

> *Trwm ar ia yw tramwy'r ôd,*
> *Trymach yw tori ammod.*

> *Heavy is the snow's assault on ice,*
> *Heavier is the breaking of a promise.*[2]

And ends as follows:

> *Y bardd bach, os dan bridd bedd*
> *Y teri hwynt i orwedd;*
> *Yn y pridd, anhap yw'r hawl,*
> *Y trig addysg tragwyddawl.*

> *If you would throw the bard*
> *Beneath the grave's soil yonder forever,*
> *In the soil, misfortune is the cause,*
> *Would everlasting learning lie*.[2]

It is in Tal-y-llyn lake that the Dysynwy starts its journey. This river, having wallowed through a variety of meadow-land and deep dark valleys for numerous miles, eventually leaves the mountain land and gushes slowly, and truly quite noisily, through the productive and

---

* This is a translation of a slightly different version of the poem, taken from J.C. Morrice's *Barddoniaeth Wiliam Llŷn* (Bangor, 1908)

fruitful plains of the district of Tywyn, past the excellent mansions of Peniarth and Ynys-y-maengwyn, until finally reaching Ceredigion (Cardigan) Bay. It is quite excellent for fish, especially the salmon, which are caught in it in large plenitude each year.

TAL-Y-WERN

A small village in the parish of Darowen, on the banks of the River Gwidol, around two miles higher up than Abercegir. There is a house of worship here owned by the Baptists. A little closer to Abercegir, below the main road, is another small village called Dol-y-bont.

TOWYN

The name given to a town and parish in the hundred of Ystumaner, Meirionnydd (Merioneth). Regarding the origin of the word, the common meaning given to it is "a place on the edge of the sea", and the name can be given to any place in just such a location; but we are a long way from being satisfied by this meaning, since the name of every place normally derives from something particular that existed in that neighbourhood. Because of this, forgive us for offering another interpretation of it.

We are informed in the *"Pedigree of the Saints"* that Saint Cadfan had an incumbent called Hywyn ap Gwyndaf who came with him from Brittany, and because Cadfan was the founder and patron of Towyn, and also an Abbot of Bardsey Island, it is likely enough that he kept an *"incumbent"* in this church, and it is more likely that that incumbent was Hywyn; and this name could easily be corrupted to "Nhywyn", and then to "Tywyn", and again to "Towyn". Also, apart from this, in the parish of Llanegryn there are two farmhouses that take the names Bod-gadfan and Bodywyn, and we can easily connect T or Tu with those names, and for those names to be corrupted to Tu Hywyn or Tywyn.

Capel Seion, Tal-y-Wern

It is commonly called Towyn Meirionnydd, in order to distinguish it from another Towyn in Caernarfonshire, which, according to the Chronicle of Princes, got its name from one Gwynn – Tŷ Gwyn.

The parish of Towyn is very large, and is bordered on its northern side by the River Dysynwy, on the western side by Ceredigion (Cardigan) Bay, and on the eastern side by the parishes of Tal-y-llyn and Pennal. It was formerly much larger than this, and included the whole of the hundred of Ystumaner. It includes around thirty-thousand acres of land, and its population in 1851 was 2764.

The small town of Towyn stands pleasantly within around a mile of the sea, near broad plains which were formerly a damp coastal marsh, and truly covered by water, with little boats floating along it, until a dyke was erected to restrain the tide. The surrounding views are extremely varied, and unite the beauties of great wilderness and charming prettiness. The houses are built mostly of the coarse grey stone of the neighbourhood, dressed in a rustic and loving kind of appearance.

Because it has such advantages as bathing places, with the smooth beach reaching for around six miles, and Cadfan's Well, which is in a field below the church and is excellent for curing articular rheumatism and other ailments, the town attracts a multitude of visitors during the summer season, especially from the western parts of Montgomeryshire. Being there during the months of July and August we truly see the hordes flowing in – some in carriages, some on horses, and some on foot – some diseased, some lame, and some unwell; some with their spirits low, with their tendons slack, and their limbs powerless, all coming there as if agreeing to forget the things that have gone past, and to hearten in the warmth of each other, until their health is *rejuvenated like the eagle*", and when they return, they return with courageous thoughts, with renewed strength, and with robustness that will woe the work put before them. And the amicable inhabitants are worthy of high commendation for the kindness and affection with which they treat all their visitors.

Because its position is in such a particular corner, in the midst of land full of agricultural resources, it appears that it once carried out significant trade, second only to Harlech in importance, holding its markets every Friday; but this was allowed to disappear, and now exists only in privilege and name.

If it relied entirely on its own resources for subsistence, it would be but dire and poor, and if it were not for its incomparable advantages as a bathing place, it is likely enough that no one would know its name thirty miles away. But because it possesses these things, the inhabitants commonly receive comfortable sustenance. They spend the winter season weaving flannels and processing wool. It is one of the places to register constituents to vote for the Member of Parliament for Meirionnydd (Merioneth). The town includes several pretty inns, apart from the large convenient and cleanly *Corbet Arms* hostel, kept by Mr W Parry, where a plenitude of horses and carriages are always ready for hire.

Popular fairs are held here on March the 16th, Easter Monday, May the 14th, September the 17th, and November the 18th.

In this town stands the church of the parish of Towyn, and it would pay well for every liker of antiquity to see it. It was built originally in the sixth century, and is dedicated to Saint Cadfan. In a song by Llewelyn Fardd a great deal is recited about the glory and splendour of the original church, and the supreme privilege of the town in having such a place of worship, but it would not serve our purpose to place it here.

It is said of Saint Cadfan, to whom the church is dedicated, that he was a son of Eneas Wledig by Gwenteirbron, the daughter of Emhyr of Brittany. It appears that he was a person of high order, and possessed extensive heirdoms in Brittany, as he was a son in law of the King of Brittany. But early in the sixth century, when the Gaulish French invaded and stole the lands owned by the Welsh there, rather than submit to the alien yoke, he sailed with a host of other saints over to his brothers in this country; and they received a welcoming reception. Cadfan established himself in Towyn, and erected a church here. After that, he was made an Abbot of Bardsey Island, to where he moved, leaving, it is likely, his incumbent, Hywyn, to service the church, from which the town received its name.

There was strife between this place and Bardsey Island regarding the grave of the Saint. The "Pedigree of the Saints" states that he was buried on Bardsey Island, while there formerly stood in Towyn cemetery a stone column around 7 feet high, with a picture of a cross and old letters, and it was always known by the name "Colofn Sant Cadfan" ("Cadfan's Column"). Although numerous drawings of the old carvings were taken, they could not be deciphered until recently; and according to the decipherment made, this confirmed the view that the body of the Saint lies here*.

The present church is built in the style of the Normans in the shape of a cross, and it is assumed from its form that it was erected around the twelfth century. The bell-tower formerly stood in the centre, but this fell in 1692, and the current tower was built on the western side in its place. It is said that the bells of the old church rang so loudly that they were heard, in a favourable breeze, twelve miles away.

The inquisitive stranger should not, on any account, go away without taking note of the old carved effigies inside. They are located on the northern side of the chancery, under rounded arches; the effigy under one arch is similar to a girdled girl, and the other is a warrior, and it is commonly presumed that it is a picture of Gruffydd Goch ap Adda, of Dolgoch in this parish. In relation to the former, some suppose it to be an emblem of Cadfan; but others think, and perhaps with more propriety, that it is of Gwenddydd, one of Brychan Brycheiniog's daughters, or perhaps of another woman called Nest, daughter of Hywel, both of whom are buried here.

The benefice is in the incumbency and vicariate of the Archdeaconry of Merioneth and the diocese of Bangor. The famous Ieuan Brydydd Hir was a curate here. Also in the town are houses of worship owned by the Calvinistic Methodists, Wesleyans, and Independents.

---

* This stone bears inscriptions thought to be the oldest written examples of the Welsh language. The stone had been used as a gate post before being brought to the church in 1761. Some translations suggest the stone marks the grave of Cingen rather than Cadfan (NIDF)

Near the town is Ynys-y-maengwyn, the residence of a long line of the Corbet family*; a very magnificent mansion in a pretty location, adorned with pleasant plants and quite ancient trees. Its gardens are amongst the best in the Principality, as they are large, and include a multitude of unusual plants and trees, amongst which are evergreen oak, which are considered amongst the fairest in the Kingdom.

During the civil war this splendid old residence was completely burnt down rather than allow it to afford any protection to the armies of the Parliament. Several years ago, near a circular mound on the land of a nearby farm called Bryn Castell, half a cannonball was found, weighing 7 pounds.

The late Edward Corbet Esq., the heir to this place, was an obliging gentleman, with a wild temper, and extremely fond of humour, and there are many jolly accounts about him fresh in the memories of the current inhabitants of the area. One excellent example of his charitable nature was his work in exacting a doctor to train him in elements of physiology, with the purpose of benefiting his tenants and the poor of the neighbourhood. Food and every care were to be had in Ynys-y-maengwyn for those who called by.

Not far from the town of Towyn, near the small village of Bryncrug, is the inconspicuous farmhouse of Glanmorfa, which was made notable as the birthplace of the genius bard Dafydd Ionawr. He was born on the 22nd of January 1751 to responsible parents, and although he had no encouragement from his father to foster his bright talents, the Lord yet looked after a gentle, loving, sensible, and religious mother to present to her the foremost tuition of the Christian chief-bard of his land; and it is certain to us that what she taught him while at the home fireside provided a pious aptitude and sacred atmosphere that influenced all his works.

Having received the first elements of his teaching in a small day

---

* See also *Rhiwsaeson* (NIDF)

school in Towyn, on the specific encouragement of the gifted and learned Ieuan Brydydd Hir, who was at that time a curate in Towyn, and who, having identified some rays of his bright gift, sent him to Ystradmeurig school, under the painstaking tutorship of Mr Edward Richards. Having stayed there for some time, he moved to Wrexham as a junior-master in the school of one Mr Tisdale; but in 1774 Dafydd moved from there to Christ's College, Oxford, with the intention of taking orders, and to adapt himself more exhaustively to the ministry. Despite this, he only stayed there one term, then returned to his old place with Mr Tisdale. Having stayed there for around three years, through his master he met a somewhat unlucky turn. We find him next as a junior-master in Caerfyrddin (Carmarthen) Grammar School. After that, in 1790, he moved to his area of birth, and got the position of teacher at the free school in Towyn, and he was there for two years. Having spent two further years publishing and selling "Cywydd y Drindod" ("*Cywydd* of the Trinity"), he went to live in Dolgellau with a kindly gentleman called Thomas Jones, where he stayed, enjoying every peace until 1800. After that he kept a free school in Dolgellau, and having spent 7 years there he gave the school up, and moved to Ynysfaig, opposite Abermaw (Barmouth) with the aforesaid Thomas Jones, where he spent many years in the greatest diligence revising his works and composing. Upon the death of his patron, in 1819, he moved again to Dolgellau, where he spent the rest of his life. We cannot identify any Welsh bard so extensive, so untainted, and, on the whole, so poetical as the "Son of Glanmorfa"; and all his work, which was recently published in a single attractive volume, with a picture of the author, will be a monument to his talent and his hard labour for all the ages of the world. He died on May the 12th 1827 in his 76th year of age.

There is a common tradition amongst the inhabitants of these domains that a rich fruitful plain, so large that it formed a

Principality on its own, formerly existed between Towyn and the sea, before the water completely covered it. To confirm this assumption, the Triads, identifying the three main drunkards of Britain[*], says

> *"Drunken Seithinyn ab Seithyn Saidi, King of Dyfed[†], who in his drunkenness let the sea over the hundred of Gwaelod so that all the houses and land which were there were lost; where there were formerly sixteen fortified towns, superior to all the towns and fortifications in Wales, with the exception of Caerllion upon Usk. The hundred of Gwaelod was a dominion of Gwyddno Garanhir, King of Ceredigion, Cantref y Gwaelod; and it was in the time of Emrys Wledig[‡] that this happened; and the men escaped from that drowning and landed in Ardudwy and the land of Arfon, and the mountains of Eryri (Snowdonia), and other places that had not been inhabited before then."*

We also have many natural proofs of this; on these coasts are numerous causeways, or large walls visible in shallow water. One of those is Sarn Badrig (Patrick's Causeway), or rather Badrhwyg, which obtrudes into the sea for many miles between Harlech and Abermaw (Barmouth), and at one end of this causeway there are sixteen large stones, one of which is four yards in diameter. We can imagine that that causeway formed one of the boundaries. The other ridges in this bay that come to view at low tide are Sarn-y-Bwch,

---

[*] The other two drunkards are referred to as follows: "First, Ceraint, the drunken king of Siluria, who in drunkenness burned all the corn far and near over all the country, so that a famine for bread arose. Second, Vortigern, who in his drink gave the Isle of Thanet to Horsa that he might commit adultery with Rowena his daughter, and who also gave a claim to the son that he had by her to the crown of Lloegria; and added to these, treachery and plotting against the Cambrians.
[†] *Dimetia* is the name given in some texts
[‡] Emrys Wledig = Ambrosius

which reaches to the sea for a mile and a half on the northern side of the mouth of the River Dysynwy; Sarn Cynfelin, which reaches seven miles out to sea from a place called Wallog, three miles to the north of Aberystwyth; the next is Sarn Dewi, reaching around a quarter of a mile out to sea, in a line, from Llanddewi church, Aberarth; the last is Sarn Cadwgan, within around a mile of Sarn Dewi, which runs over a mile and a half out to sea[*]. In addition to this, numerous large tree stumps are found low in the sand on these coasts, and a few years ago the antiquarian Llwyd stated that he had seen a considerable number of oak trees at low tide close to the estuary of the River Dysynwy, and the trunk of one of these trees was six foot in diameter. Nor did the early Welsh bards leave this completely unnoted; there is also a very magnificent old song in which are named many of the towns and rivers in Cantref y Gwaelod, as well as an elaborate portrait of the country and the lively quality of the inhabitants.

Here are the proofs we have of the existence of such a tract of land as Cantref y Gwaelod, and it is firm enough, I believe, to establish the fact beyond fiction.

But that

> *"Seithinyn was a drunk*
> *For his unprovoked betrayal"*

is a question we cannot easily come to a decision on, although we do not doubt for a minute that a man could complete such a heinous deed under the influence of intoxicating drink, if it was within his capability; nevertheless, it is not easy to imagine that the situation of Cantref y Gwaelod was so insecure that one man, much less a drunk man, could cause such unavoidable destruction to such a large land. And, allowing that the surface of the sea was a lot higher than the

---

[*] Morgan's Guide to Aberdovey, page 57

land in this place, and that walls and great banks were built to defend it, as can be seen presently in many coastal parts of the Netherlands, for what purpose were flood-gates mentioned? And if so, is it likely that one or a few men could open them? It is far more believable to me that the waters rushed in with the ferment of a hurricane, and broke a gap in the barrage until it opened a way for a demolishing flow to stream in over the whole country, such as we had an example of a few years ago in the Netherlands.

Also, perhaps these waters did not come upon the whole of the country at once, but could have taken land despite the creation of the world, and buried the occasional town in its turn, if there were inhabitants alive there. It is an undeniable fact that the sea continues to take land in these parts; within the memory of old people recently alive, the current beach was once fields, and they remembered harvesting plentiful crops of corn on them, and by the estuary of the River Dysynwy it has gained several hundred yards of land in the last century, and if it took only a few hundred more, it could run unbarred through the whole region of Towyn, burying the current town in a watery grave. Indeed, there is a tradition amongst the inhabitants that the old town of Towyn was built some miles further to the west than the current one, and that it met the same fate as Cantref y Gwaelod. We have proven that the bay of Ceredigion (Cardigan) is continuing to come further inland, and it is likely that it will come in further until it reaches the "foothills of the mountains".

TRE'RDDOL

A village in the parish of Llancynfelyn, standing on a pleasant plain half-way between Machynlleth and Aberystwyth. The houses are

A meet of the Gogerddan Foxhounds at Lodge Park,
or 'Coed-y-lodge'

scattered in irregular batches each side of the River Clettwr. Its name derives from the large flat meadow that is near the place.

The main calling of the inhabitants is hard hat manufacturing, and bearing them the length of the country to sell.

It contains two inns; the *Halfway House* and the *Dolclettwr Arms*. In the north-easterly end of the village there is a pretty house of worship, with a graveyard by it, owned by the Calvinistic Wesleyans. The road that leads from Eglwysfach to Tre'rddol is wooded and shady. Within less than a mile of the latter is *Coed-y-lodge*, the property of Pryse Loveden Esq., MP, Gogerddan. It is a large beech-wood, running by the side of the road for half a mile. These trees have been a place of fright for the inhabitants around, and have scared wretched travellers who passed; for some "ghost" would trick them here in the night. It is said that it was very *"angry"* once, but that some wizard or other succeeded in putting it *"down"* some time ago. Travellers will remember this as a comfort while going past the

155

place – that the restless one has been bound!

TRE'TALIESIN

A village a mile further on than the former. There are numerous houses in orderly rows on each side of the road, numerous inns and shops, and a post-office, which is kept by Mr Thomas Jones.

The author of these lines heard an old man say that he remembered the place with only three houses in it. The name of the place at that time was *"Comins-y-Dfarn-fach"*. Before, the place was open land (common), but when this was sold by the *Commissioners,* through the *"Act of Enclosure"* which applied to it and to Cors-fochno, the land on which the village stands was bought by one Morris Davies from Aberystwyth, who gave leases to build houses upon it, and the three individual houses were soon surrounded by a horde of new houses; and because the grave of old Taliesin, the head of the bards, was on a nearby hill, it was decided that the place from thereon would be called Tre' Taliesin. The village has, since a short while ago, become more important through the rich land-works (mines) that are in the neighbourhood. The inhabitants come by their fuel, namely peat, on Cors Fochno, which is nearby, between this area and the sea.

There is a chapel owned by the Calvinistic Methodists here. When they started building this chapel, it is said of an old woman who, because of zeal and faithfulness, would walk around a mile (of road) many times in one day to bring stones for the building, carrying them there on her head!

Because the name Taliesin is so associated with this place, and his remains lay so close to it, perhaps a few notes about the *"Head of the*

156

Bards of the West" would not be unacceptable to the reader.

The place and time of Taliesin's birth are not certain; but it is the common view that the main period of his life was between the years 520 and 570. It is said in the *"Mabinogion"* that he was a son of Tegid Foel from Benllyn, near Llyn Tegid, by his wife Ceridwen, who was a sorceress. After this, we are completely in the dark regarding his background, until he was found in a fishing-weir.

The legend of his godsend is recounted as follows:- After the water had covered Cantref y Gwaelod*, and the circumstances of Gwyddno Garanhir, its last principal, had become uncomfortable, the only thing he could do towards his own, and his son, Elphin's, preservation was to form a fishing-weir near the village of Borth. It appears that the contraption had not proved to be very productive for some spell, but one afternoon the keeper of the weir came to Elphin and informed him that a coracle containing a live child had been caught, and, presenting the child to him, he said "Behold this fair catch/behold this fair forehead" - "Taliesin will be his name" said Elphin. The meaning of this is *talcen iesin = fair forehead* or *beautiful.*

Elphin behaved towards him as an honourable and Christian Prince. After he had patronised and tutored him for a lengthy period, his patron took him to the court of his father Gwyddno, and, on this occasion, the bard, while only a small boy, presented his secret song to the old Principal, namely "The Story of Taliesin", which starts as follows:-

> *Prif fardd cyffredin wyf fi i Elphin;*
> *A'm bro gysefin yw gwlad Cerubin;*
> *Johannes ddewin a'm galwes i Merddin;*
> *Bellach pob brenin a'm geilw Taliesin*
> *&c.*

---

* See *Towyn*

157

I am Elphin's fair chief-bard;
And my foremost land is Cerubin's country;
Johannes the sorcerer named me Merddin;
Now every king calls me Taliesin
&c.[2]

And to his kind benefactors he presented an extraordinarily graceful and touching song, to comfort them in the face of their failure, and in which he endeavoured, with exceptional deftness, to move away his deep sadness and heartbreaking sorrow. It was called "Elphin's consolation", and it starts like this:

Elphin dêg, taw a'th wylo,
Na chabled neb yr eiddo;
Ni wna les drwg-obeithio;
Ni ŵyl dyn ddim a'i porthio;
Ni bydd coeg gweddi Cynllo;
Ni thŷr Dyw ar addawo;
Ni chaed yn nghored Wyddno
Erioed cystal a heno
&c.

Fair Elphin cease your weeping,
Let no one be dissatisfied with his lot,
To anticipate bad will bring no benefit.
No man sees what carries him;
The prayer of Cynllo will not be empty;
God will not go back on his promise;
Never in Gwyddno's wear was had
As good as tonight.
&c.

After he had grown to an appropriate age, he was sent to Llancarfan Monastery, the teaching place of Catwg Doeth (Wise Catwg). While here he became acquainted with Urien Rheged, the Prince of the northern part of England, who took him into his family, where he received the companionship of the immortal bard Aneurin, and the visionary Merddin Wyllt (Wild Merlin).

After some period of time it appears that he left Urien, and went into the service of his calling in the court of Maelgwyn Gwynedd. While there, he had a fair opportunity to repay the gifts he had received at the hand of his original patron; due to some unknown quarrel, Elphin was imprisoned by his uncle, Maelgwyn Gwynedd, in Deganwy Castle, and this incensed Taliesin to compose a song to present to the Prince on behalf of his old benefactor; and he was successful, not only in terms of securing Elphin's freedom, but also in elevating himself to more attention and favour with Maelgwyn.

Through his friendship with Maelgwyn he received a small patronage from him, that he could retire to when he wished, and according to some lines of his estate we can imagine that this was by Llyn Geirionydd, in the parish of Llanrhychwyn, Caernarvonshire, hence:

A minau Taliesin
O lan Llyn Geirionydd

And me Taliesin
From the banks of Llyn Geirionydd

Taliesin did not spurn the happiness of family life; he married, and had a son, on whom the mantle of his father did not fall. Nevertheless, he did his best, and the only line of his work that is kept in memory runs in a mournful tone, communicating the pain of composing, and to appease us with the loss of the rest,

A glywaist ti a gânt Afaon
Fab Taliesin, gerdd gyfion? –
　　'Ni chel grudd gystudd calon'

Did you hear what Afaon sang
Taliesin's son, in remembered verse?
　　'The Cheek cannot hide the afflicted heart'

But Afaon put the harp down to take up the lance, and was one of the bravest and notable warriors of his time. He is counted as one of the *"three battle bulls of the island of Britain"* *, and also one of the *"three grave slaughterers who avenged their wrongs from their graves[†]."*

Not only was Taliesin exceptional as a bard, but it is supposed that he also held some position associated with the Druidic religion, which, so it is thought, gave him the right to the title "Head Bard", and it does not appear that one of the former Welsh bards so familiar with him was in the druidic mysteries.

All his compositions have been heavily steeped in references from nature, which are, by now, almost incomprehensible; and if this was not to be seen from his compositions, we have his own definitive testimony on the matter:

Myfi Taliesin
A wn bob gorsin yn ngogof gor-ddewin

---

* According to Iolo Morganwg, Afaon was in fact one of the three *Bull Princes* of the Isle of Britain, the other two being Elmur, the adopted son of Cibddar, and Cynhafel son of Argad. The three bulls of battle of the Isle of Britain were Cynfar Cadgadawg, son of Cynwyd Cynwydion; Gwendolleu, son of Ceidaw; and Urien, son of Cynfarch, because they rushed upon their foes like bulls, and it was not possible to avoid them.
[†] The other two grave slaughterers were Selyf, son of Cynan Garwyn, and Gwallawg, son of Lleenawg.

It is I Taliesin
Who knows every margin in the cave of the sorcerer

This, according to learned judgement, points to his thorough knowledge of the secrets of the arch-druid, and it sometimes appears that this is boastful testimony by him. Nevertheless, it is likely that he received the type of Christian impression on his thinking from his tutor Catwg Ddoeth (Wise Catwg) such that he came to a broadly correct view of true belief, and some of his compositions that are available prove that he was worthy to be listed as one of the *"three Christian Head-Bards of the island of Britain"*.

There are about forty songs available that take his name, and although it is not possible to say that all of them belong to him, we nevertheless sincerely believe that most of them are, which is strong testimony to the fertility of his genius, for it is reasonable to conclude from the consideration that as so many of them did not get lost or vanish in such a prolonged period, those that have reached our age are only a small proportion of his compositions. But the greatest fragment amongst all his works is the one called *"The Prophecy of Taliesin"*, which doubtless articulates that while every Welshman breaths:

> *Eu Ner a folant;*
> *Eu hiaith a gadwant*
> *Eu tir a gollant*
> > *Ond Gwyllt Walia*

> *Their God they will praise*
> *Their language they will keep*
> *Their land they will lose*
> > *Except for Wild Wales*

The common view is that Taliesin died around the year 570. His memory has been kept exceedingly revered by his countrymen throughout the ages. Tradition has it that he spent his last days in the old area where he received his early nurture and culture, and his grave is apparently not far from Tre' Taliesyn, on a hill called Pen-sarn-ddu (Top of the black causeway), between the Rivers Ceulan and Clettwr. It comprises a large piece of land with two lines of stones around it, the furthest out is 31 feet in diameter, and the other 27 feet. The mound is commonly called "Gwely Taliesin", but recently some unscrupulous scoundrel destroyed this cairn, unloosened the coffin-stone, and treated the bones like an accursed thing. For inside were found bones, and even a human skull, which, it seems likely, belonged to the *"Head-Bard of the West"*.

TWYMYN

This crystal river originates on the mountains of Dylifau, and, having poured in a torrent over a high rock close to its origin, flows through the fertile valley of Pennant, Llanbrynmair. By Tafolwern it joins with quite a large river, and rolls further through a deep wooded valley, along a rocky bed, past Commins Coch, until it discharges into the Dyfi by Doldwymyn. Its fish are numerous, sizeable, and delicious.

UWCHYGARREG

A tithe-township in the parish of Machynlleth, six miles to the southeast of the town. It includes the highest part of the parish, and the land is commonly peaty and infertile. The population in 1851 was 379.

YSTUMANER

A hundred in the county of Meirionnydd (Merioneth). Some assume that the meaning of the name is *pose of the heifer*[*], because it is assumed that it bears some resemblance to the form of that animal; but others argue that it is the pose of aran, or Aran y Gesail, a high mountain around which the hundred stands, and a corruption of that word, through being spoken or written in haste, is ystumaner, just as "Eshog" is often spoken "Esgob". The law courts associated with this hundred are held every month in Pennal, Aberdyfi, and pivotally in Tywyn.

CARADAWG O LANCARFAN

---

[*] Ystum = pose or meander

164

REFERENCES TO POETRY TRANSLATIONS

1   Dafydd Johnston (Editor), *Iolo Goch: Poems,* Gomer Press, 1993
2   Eurig Salisbury, © 2007
3   Joseph P. Clancy (Editor), *Medieval Welsh Poems,* Four Courts Press, 2003.
4   Joseph P. Clancy, *The Earliest Welsh Poetry* (Edinburgh, 1970

INDEX*

---

* This index is based upon the original contents pages of *Darlundraeth o Fachynlleth a'i Hamgylchoedd*, and, as in all other parts of this book, preserves the original spellings used by the author (NIDF)